Quarterly Essay

Quarterly Essay is published four times a year by Black Inc., an imprint of Schwartz Publishing Pty Ltd. Publisher: Morry Schwartz.

ISBN 978-1-86395-716-8 ISSN 1832-0953

Subscriptions – 1 year (4 issues): $59 within Australia incl. GST. Outside Australia $89.
2 years (8 issues): $105 within Australia incl. GST. Outside Australia $165.

Payment may be made by Mastercard or Visa, or by cheque made out to Schwartz Publishing. Payment includes postage and handling.

To subscribe, fill out and post the subscription card or form inside this issue, or subscribe online:
www.quarterlyessay.com
subscribe@blackincbooks.com
Phone: 61 3 9486 0288

Correspondence should be addressed to:

The Editor, Quarterly Essay
37–39 Langridge Street
Collingwood VIC 3066 Australia
Phone: 61 3 9486 0288 / Fax: 61 3 9486 0244
Email: quarterlyessay@blackincbooks.com

Editor: Chris Feik. Management: Sophy Williams, Caitlin Yates. Publicity: Anna Lensky. Design: Guy Mirabella. Assistant Editor: Kirstie Innes-Will. Production Coordinator: Siân Scott-Clash. Typesetting: Duncan Blachford.

Printed by Griffin Press, Australia. The paper used to produce this book comes from wood grown in sustainable forests.

For my family, past, present and future.
And for Lisa Mitchell, finest clinician and friend.

DEAR LIFE | On Caring for the Elderly

Karen Hitchcock

> We elders have learned a thing or two, including invisibility …
> When I mention the phenomenon to anyone around my age, I get
> back nods and smiles. Yes, we're invisible. Honored, respected, even
> loved, but not quite worth listening to anymore. You've had your
> turn, Pops; now it's ours.
>
> — Roger Angell, 93

There are many ways to get sick, many ways to crumble and crash. I
work as a physician in a big inner-city hospital overflowing with the sick.
The orthopaedic ward is full of people who got up for a glass of water
and snapped their hip. The psychiatry ward's full of near suicides and
phantom voices drilling holes in people's heads. The cardiac cath lab's
overflowing with heart attacks. The burns unit usually has one or two
people who tipped a bucket of petrol over their head and struck a match.
We house the frail and the elderly, the drunken and overdosed. Hearts
and lungs are plucked from the brain-dead and sewn into the diseased;
people crowd the emergency department, suffering because their organs
are slowly failing the body that shelters them. What made them sick?

What is health? What is it that we do to people in a hospital?

Fundamentally, it would seem, a doctor's job is to treat and protect diseased and threatened organs – those beautiful and intricate and faithful structures that pump and squeeze and metabolise away, mostly quietly, keeping us alive. Just treat them, doc, and go home. How difficult can it be? But when doctors sit in consulting rooms or walk the wards, we don't confront kidneys and hearts. We encounter complex, imperfect, suffering people with specific histories, cultures and understandings of sickness and health. And we do this, for the most part, within institutions with vast management structures whose role is to maintain economic viability and safety. We do it within government-dictated fiscal constraints. The business of health care is something much more than a delivery of goods and services.

The medical system is constructed from tacked-together fragments – GP, specialists, the hospital, mental health services, community services – all of which have little contact with each other. We treat social and medical needs separately, although they are intricately entwined. Hospitals themselves are designed around a body fragmented into discrete organs. Often, our institutions serve clinicians, bureaucrats and cutting-edge science better than those they are supposed to be serving.

Most of my patients are old. This new longevity of ours is a triumph. I have had patients who are over 100 years of age and still live at home. I see them and feel wonder and hope. But the health system – and society – is struggling to adapt to our ageing population. At times it seems we are struggling against it.

In 1976 Robert Neil Butler, an American geriatrician, won a Pulitzer Prize for his book *Why Survive? Being old in America*, in which he coined the term "ageism." In *Why Survive?* Butler outlines many ways the elderly are neglected in society and shut out of the medical system. Five years earlier, in France, Simone de Beauvoir published *The Coming of Age*, in which she too describes a society where the elderly are forgotten, discarded or despised. Both books are rigorously researched and statistic-heavy. The points the writers make are as relevant today as they were forty years ago.

It is difficult to improve the care we offer our elders – in and out of hospital – when, as Linda Marsa writes, we are fearful of "the swelling ranks of 'greedy geezers', the oncoming grey tsunami of the sick and frail elderly who will be an emotional and financial burden on their families and friends, and whose infirmities could bankrupt the healthcare system." We hear a continual cry that our healthcare system is "unsustainable"; that the healthcare needs of ageing baby-boomers may bankrupt the country. Age discrimination in medicine is widespread, although often hidden behind many benevolent aims: the promotion of patient auton-omy, the wise allocation of health resources, the avoidance of what is futile, the primacy of quality of life. Our response to age-related memory loss and dementia is to institutionalise, isolate, sedate. Supporting inde-pendence and wellbeing in old age remains a low priority.

One of the most-read articles in the *Atlantic* in 2014 was "Why I Hope to Die at 75" by a professor of bioethics, Ezekiel Emanuel. In it, he jauntily promotes the idea that it is a horror to grow old; that growing old neces-sarily involves the accumulation of disability, the transformation of a human subject into a wreck and a burden on family and society. Ema-nuel's answer to his dire evaluation of elderly life is to die early. There's a picture of him, a man in his late fifties, radiating vitality, sitting with his feet up on his desk, long legs crossed, drinking from a cup that says "The Boss." Another picture shows him with his arms slung around two of his nephews at a base camp of Mount Kilimanjaro, which the three climbed. Accompanying the article is a bright yellow graph that depicts the decline in one's productivity with increasing age. Emanuel knows his place – as the boss, at the top of the mountain, at the peak of a very particular kind of productivity – and he would rather die than give it up.

There are many ways to show that we devalue our elderly, are repulsed by them, terrified of becoming them. They have been and remain the last priority in our medical system and the ones we target first with our auster-ity measures. This essay does not offer simple solutions to the structural inadequacies it diagnoses. The solutions are not simple. My chief aim is to strike a note of caution and to make explicit something that often remains unsaid and yet can be heard quite clearly: that the elderly are burdensome, bankrupting, non-productive. That old age is not worth living.

Before I started studying medicine, my grandmother was diagnosed with idiopathic pulmonary fibrosis. I had no idea what that was.

"Scarring of the lungs," she said.

She was put on little white tablets called prednisolone. I had no idea what they were.

She was thrilled when I announced my plan to become a doctor. She was ecstatic with pride. She'd tell anyone who listened – the person scanning our groceries at the supermarket, for example. She'd look at him, then at me, then at him and I'd know it was coming: "This is my granddaughter."

The guy would look up from the tin of baked beans in his hand, his face all, "*And?*"

She'd put her hand on my forearm, lean in towards him and say, "She's studying to be a doctor."

I'd roll my eyes and go, "Nan, jeez ..."

When I visited her at home, the first thing she'd say to me as I walked in the door was, "Stop. Stand over there. Now turn around."

I'd roll my eyes and say, "Nan, jeez."

"I just want to look at you," she'd say. "Now, come here, and bring that comb." She'd been a hairdresser. My hair often didn't live up to her standards.

In my second year of med school, I bought my first stethoscope. When Nan said, "Stand over there," I said, "Wait!" Pulled the stethoscope out of my backpack, looped it around my neck and turned around. You should have seen her face.

By the time I was in third year, she was eighty-one and permanently attached by the nostrils to a long tube connected to an oxygen concentrator. The concentrator sat in the lounge room, humming like an air-conditioner, and the tube was long enough for her to move all around the house.

She said, "My lungs are 'diseased', what a terrible word … Listen to them if you wish."

I pressed my stethoscope against her soft pink skin, and caught my breath. By then I knew what those fine crackling sounds meant.

She always had an afternoon nap, and I'd get into bed next to her with my textbook, and she'd quietly watch me from her side of the twenty or so pillows.

Just before my fourth-year clinical exams, she fell in the bathroom at night and lay on the cold tiles until morning. At the hospital they said she'd had a heart attack and things looked bad. She was too weak to drink. She gripped my hand, hard as steel, and whispered to me, "I don't want to die yet."

The consultant physician said, "We could consider palliation …"

I begged him, "Please keep going."

In hospital she told me halting, dreamy stories, about planting the orchard of almond trees on the bare land her husband inherited in Deer Park. How the neighbouring farmers laughed at her and said, "Almonds won't grow here, love. It's futile." She watered them by hand, with buckets when there was no rain, watched them grow. I'd spent my childhood gathering sacks of nuts from those gigantic trees.

One evening Nan's IV cannula blocked and the cover resident came to site a new one, a trainee nurse in tow. I don't know what the IV line was for – fluid or diuretics or antibiotics – something necessary for her treatment. The resident said to me authoritatively, "You realise this is futile." I tried to explain – that, for Nan, being in hospital and the pain of a thin needle in her forearm was worth it for a little more life – but it came out as a stutter. I just stood there under his accusatory stare, gripped by deep shame.

He told me to wait in the corridor. I heard him croon to my Nan, as she winced with each of his failed attempts: "I'm sorry, you poor thing. This is cruel. We know it's unfair." There was silence for a moment. "Let's try the cubital fossa," he said to the nurse, and then started chatting with her about his plans for surgical training. When they were done, they walked out and past me without a word. I went back in, pressed my cheek against my grandmother's cool forehead and said I was sorry.

"Don't worry ..." she said, stroking my hair. "Everything's okay."

*

Some doctors seem to view old patients as a different species of human, unrelated in any way to their young selves.

At every morning handover in every hospital in Australia, a registrar will report admitting an elderly patient – perhaps a 92-year-old who fell taking out the garbage – and say, "He's so cute" or "She's so adorable." As if the patient were a baby or a kitten. This doesn't seem so terrible. It is not meant to be cruel or disparaging. But what does it tell us about the way we view the elderly?

If you are old and in hospital, you can be one of three things: cute, difficult or mute. If you want people to be nice to you, I'd recommend cute. It's easy to be cute: just say something any normal human might say. Because you are ancient, it will be seen as cute. If you want the best treatment and don't give a damn whom you piss off, be difficult. It's not hard to be difficult: simply respond as one should when a 25-year-old speaks to you as if you are three. Alternatively, request that you get your bedpan within half an hour and that your tea be hot.

I looked after two "difficult" patients in the same week last year. The word peppered their medical histories. Elizabeth was in her nineties, had higher degrees in the liberal arts and had worked as a curator in Australia and Europe. She was not so much difficult as grumpy: seething at the suggestion that she be placed in care, that she had to share a room with a man, that her preferences for various aspects of her care were inconvenient, that she was in hospital instead of visiting the Aztecs exhibition at the museum. Geraldine, also in her nineties, had been a highly respected historian. She was difficult in her refusal to have her blood pressure taken several times a day, her selective adherence to her medication regimen and her determination to walk to the toilet by herself.

Perhaps you might as well be mute. You're in an anonymous white gown, in a strange bed, your hair is grey, your facial features are desiccated. Who the hell knows who you are? You are old. Enough said.

It is not that doctors are particularly cruel or stupid or insensitive. On the contrary, they are more often smart and hard-working and very kind. But we all reflect and are shaped by our culture. This is the way many people think of the elderly, if we think of them at all, which many people do not unless they see a headline about how they're threatening the financial future of our great and productive country: sucking up our health resources, burdening families, spending their kids' inheritance on motor scooters so they can get to the TAB, crumbling and leaking and bent over, gripping their walking sticks with big white knuckles, staring at us askance as we slip into the last seat on the tram.

And now here they are — half-naked, a bit loopy with disorientation after a night travelling from ambulance to emergency department to ward — and we're all over them, up close when they are still covered in blood and vomit and stinking of a urinary tract infection.

It is confronting and terrifying to see one's own future up close like this. To be hit day after day with the reality of decline and death, to see fear and pain: the kind you feel powerless to address, let alone ameliorate. And even if you wanted to, who has the time? Most medical wards — particularly in the winter — are running on the junior doctors' unpaid overtime. They haven't the time to eat, let alone start a conversation about how terribly isolated the 86-year-old in bed 18 might be. It's all "What's the chest X-ray show?" and "Is he allergic to ceftriaxone?" and "Book him into sub-acute or rehab ASAP." Because down in the emergency department they just keep on coming.

If you are an elderly patient's family, you also have choices. You can be reasonable (you agree with us) or unreasonable (you do not). Some unreasonable families demand active treatment for their sick family member, who may or may not be dying. The alternative to active treatment is to provide "comfort measures only," to "palliate": that is, to not treat or investigate the disease, but to ensure the patient does not suffer as they die.

I recall one particularly unreasonable family who felt a registrar had bullied them into accepting palliation for their father. He had long-standing lung disease and obstructive sleep apnoea, and his carbon dioxide levels tended to be high. Because of these higher-than-normal carbon dioxide levels, when he became sick and his breathing slowed, he would get drowsy. He came to the emergency department drowsy and was put on an NIV (non-invasive ventilation) breathing mask for a few hours (a treatment that can lower carbon dioxide levels). He failed to wake up. The medical registrar thought he should not receive any more NIV, and should go to the ward to receive "comfort measures only": that is, be palliated. His son disagreed. His son said that he told everyone who'd listen, "He always gets like this when he's sick. He always gets better with the mask. It just takes time."

The patient woke up overnight on the ward and when I went to meet him for the first time in the morning, he smiled and asked me, "Do you think I'll get home by Friday? It's my birthday and I want to dance." He twirled his hands and laughed.

*

Many years ago, as a first-year registrar, I saw a patient named Eric in the emergency department. He was mumbling incoherent words, in respiratory distress, his entire body swollen with fluid his heart could no longer move through his blood vessels. His wife sat on the edge of the seat beside the bed, kneading her handbag strap. Eric had advanced heart failure and had been admitted to hospital every month or two for the past year. Each time he came in, he'd be dried out and discharged home on medications he refused to take and a fluid restriction he could not tolerate – so he'd rapidly become swollen and short of breath again, and his wife would bring him back to hospital. I knew the medical treatment that would bring him back to his baseline and could give it. But why wasn't he taking his medication? Why couldn't he limit his intake of fluids?

I asked Eric's wife what was happening at home and she started to cry. He hadn't been coherent for months. When he spoke, he was aggressive and lashed out at her verbally and physically. He hadn't caused her harm, as he was quite weak, but she cowered as she described their life together. He screamed at her if she tried to limit his fluid intake, and threw his pills at her. He said he just wanted to be left alone.

I offered her sympathy, and went to make her a cup of tea so I could think. When I came back, I said, "We could stop."

She looked at her husband in the bed, she looked at me.

I said, "Maybe we could let him be, treat his breathlessness with low doses of morphine and just see?"

I felt dizzy. It was the first time I had ever suggested palliation for a patient.

She wiped her eyes and whispered, "I think that would be good."

I was full of panic. Was it the right thing to let him die? He was unable to make decisions for himself, but he had repeatedly refused treatment, and both he and his wife were in a wretched state. She'd refused numerous times to let him be placed in a care facility, but things were getting worse. I walked to the phone, and rang the on-call physician.

The physician said, "What you are telling me is this is a patient who wants us to leave him alone, yes?"

I chewed my nails, my inner cheek, my lips. "But he doesn't know what he's doing. We could treat him," I said.

"With what aim?"

"I don't know. Perhaps there is a way to improve their situation?"

"How?" he asked.

*

"What's the point?" I frequently hear people say. "What sort of life is that?" Eric's is an extreme example, probably the worst I've seen: a conflagration of dementia, organ dysfunction and a lifetime of aggressive behaviour. But I am often told stories of people's family members struggling or drifting aimlessly through their last years of life – if not suffering, then living what seems to the storyteller an empty existence. Unable to walk to the shops. Taking ten pills a day. Isolated. Housebound. Sitting for two years in a nursing home, waiting to die. This is often the introduction to a defence of euthanasia, an attack on medicine: *what is the point?* But there is no answer to that existential question. There may be no point to anyone's life, or there may be many points. Often, on further questioning, it emerges that the elderly family member has never themselves expressed a desire to die, has never themselves asked, "What is the point?" Often it is not the elderly person who is suffering physical or emotional discomfort; it is their family.

There are two strong narratives in our culture about the ageing population and death. The first is that medicine is keeping elderly patients alive against their will – medicine is denying a death that the patient desires. The second is that elderly patients are seeking to stay alive unreasonably – the patient (or their family) is denying an unavoidable death.

In response to these narratives, there are calls for us – doctors, patients, the general population – to accept death, confront it and prepare for it, as if this is straightforward, as if death is not, for many, a horrifying proposition, as if it is not natural for us to turn from the fact of our own demise.

I have woken many times in the deep silence of the night, filled with the realisation that one day I will die. The thought – recognised and held in my imagination for a fleeting moment – fills me with terror, makes my limbs weak with fear: I will cease to exist. Then the sun comes up, I step out of bed into the light and the bustling music of living – my children's chatter, traffic, birds, the boiling kettle – and the knowledge is again suppressed. That we find it impossible to hold on to the fact of our own effacement is not abnormal; it is natural. It may even be what enables us to have a life. It is difficult for us to think about our own death, except as a kind of puppet show, with ourselves watching as a spectator. To fear and abhor it is rational. We only die once; there's no scope to practise: it is the abyss. Recommendations that we accept death, bring it into life, see it as natural, discuss it openly and frequently – these are easily uttered platitudes that ignore what it is to be human. In some ways, they too are a denial: of the enormity of death.

And in the hospital we do talk about death – obliquely or directly – all the time. Forms are filled out the moment people arrive in the emergency department, outlining limitations to treatment: if your heart stops, if you can no longer breathe, if you start to die, what should we do? We mark patients as "not for cardiopulmonary resuscitation," "not for intubation or intensive care" or "try everything."

In the 1990s the UK National Health Service (NHS) adopted a care plan for dying patients: the Liverpool Care Pathway for the Dying Patient (LCP or Liverpool pathway). It was rolled out to all public hospitals, so that inexpert doctors and nurses had a generic guide to follow as a patient died. A single chart covered care for a patient's physical, emotional, social and spiritual needs. The NHS financially rewarded hospitals each time they used the pathway.

It soon emerged that there were serious problems with the ways this tool was used by individual doctors and nurses. In 2013, after critical media reports and numerous complaints from the families of patients who had died – or not died – on the pathway, the government commissioned a House of Lords review. The outcome was a report entitled *More Care, Less Pathway* and withdrawal of the Liverpool protocol. Chief among the review's findings were that elderly patients were often placed on the pathway when they had treatable medical conditions, junior doctors placed people on the pathway without senior input, death was often hastened through the inappropriate use of high doses of sedatives, patients were denied food and drink when they requested it, and training and levels of staffing were utterly inadequate. Thousands of patients who may have lived, died.

The aim of the Liverpool protocol was benevolent, its goals sound. And yet it had a fatal flaw, a single thing that was not taken into account: age discrimination. For some doctors, an elderly patient who was sick might as well have been dead, and to put them on a pathway to death had become relatively easy – a tick-box exercise. While the protocol contained a note to the effect that the diagnosis of dying, the declaration of futility, is neither simple nor clear, those instituting the protocol's wide adoption failed to fully appreciate the consequences of the fact that doctors are fallible human beings whose decisions are influenced by their own values and prejudices. That how a tool is applied depends upon the individual wielding the tool; that it might easily become a weapon. In Australia, as in the UK, there is evidence that the problem is not that we never allow patients to die, but that we may declare a situation hopeless when it may not be so.

*

A nurse called the medical response team for an elderly patient who had come to hospital after falling and breaking her arm. The patient was delirious and calling out in pain. The ICU doctor looked at her, decided on palliative management and called the palliative care team to come and start a morphine and midazolam infusion (potent pain and sedative medications delivered subcutaneously to relieve the suffering of the dying).

I was the medical registrar attending and went to read the patient's notes. On arrival, she'd had basic blood tests, which showed signs that she might have an infection. No one had looked for the source of the infection – though an infection may have precipitated her fall and been contributing to her delirium. The palliative care nurse and I looked at each other.

"Maybe we're jumping the gun here?" I said.

"Seriously," the nurse said.

We cancelled the "for palliative management only" order, got the nurses to take a urine sample, gave the patient pain relief and when the urine test came back positive for infection, started antibiotics.

I wonder if the main problem, the first problem, is not that we deny death, but that we deny the entire thing: that we will grow old, that we will be like them. We ask our colleagues to shoot us if we ever get like that, and say we wish to die before we hit seventy-five.

The health needs of the old were virtually ignored until those needs started to cost us money. If this were not the case, if we saw the elderly as valuable members of society and our future selves – rather than infantilised creatures, leaking from every orifice, their past and their features macerated and blurred – we would not treat them in the ways we do: failing to provide community supports to extend independence, letting them starve in hospitals ill-designed to house them, letting them languish in emergency departments for twenty-four hours while we attend to those we consider more important. Why is it so difficult for so many of us to look at an 80-year-old and see an individual? What is it that we are denying?

Our collective turning away from ageing is reflected and concentrated in the hospital, as this is where the sick and the dying aged come for help, where the most extreme and skewed visions of what it means to be old – and the low priority we have placed on the wellbeing of the elderly – can be most clearly perceived. It is in our institutions (hospitals, nursing homes) that our culture-wide neglect is made manifest.

There are increasing numbers of ageing citizens who require health and pension services. There is general and growing fear that this will lead to worldwide financial disaster. This perception has infiltrated our health systems and has led to a number of movements within medicine that are either consciously or unconsciously informed by our low regard for the elderly and the fiscal fear they now embody. Some of these movements – advanced planning, dying with dignity, avoiding futile over-treatment – are morally sound and even laudable, but given our cultural climate they risk giving sanction to a form of health-rationing for our elderly, in a system which historically has held them in the lowest regard.

FRAGMENTS

A hospital is a place where a sick individual and their loved ones are taken in and shoved up against a group of strangers – clinicians – with whom they develop a relationship which is hugely intimate and has difficulties on both sides.

Most of the patients now entering hospitals suffer from more than one physical problem; they are older, and have complex social circumstances that need to be addressed. A patient may have pneumonia that has stressed their heart, which has in turn affected their kidney and liver function. Many suffer delirium as a consequence of infection or pain, or simply from being moved from their usual surrounds. The ravages caused by life-long diabetes are starting to manifest. Diligently taking ten different pre-scribed medications has made them very sick. Their ability to cope at home is a precariously balanced tower of circumstance and luck.

What happens when these patients present to an emergency depart-ment? Who grants them entry to the institution and decides which bed, which ward, they end up in and which doctors will care for them? It may surprise you to hear that when your mother or your grandfather presents to a hospital, his or her arrival may set off a turf war. Doctors won't fight to take care of him; they'll fight not to.

In the last half of the twentieth century, as these "multi-morbid" patients became more common, medicine at the hospital level became more specialised. Cardiologists, respiratory physicians, neurologists, nephrologists and endocrinologists gradually replaced the generalist phy-sician. Each organ had its expert, and if you came to hospital with a prob-lem in that organ, its expert would welcome you. This specialisation contributed greatly to our knowledge of the workings of the human body, and to our knowledge of disease; it led to medical marvels such as organ transplantation. Greater knowledge, technology and expertise brought with it the super-specialists: cardiologists who only treat heart failure, or arrhythmias, or only do angiograms, or only treat patients with heart transplants. And if you have an otherwise robust body with an arrhythmic heart or you need a transplant, you should be glad the experts exist. If you come to hospital with florid thyrotoxicosis, you'll be fine: an endocrinologist will look after your thyroid gland with punctilious attention.

But what if you come with two or three or four organs failing, and can no longer negotiate your stairs to go and buy food? What if your disease won't fit into a fragment? Who will be your doctor?

Hospitals had become the institutions of a utopian world where medicine had the cure for every ill, for a human being split into organs that would fail in an organised fashion. The old general physicians, the in-hospital specialists who would treat the multi-organ failures, the decrepit and the mysterious, had been rendered obsolete. At the same time, the geriatricians – specialists in the care of the elderly – did not as a rule work in acute hospital units. They would consult on problems such as frequent falls and dementia, and run outpatient clinics and rehabilitation facilities, but they were rarely on the wards.

In 1997, from an English department in Melbourne, I applied to medical school at the University of Newcastle. I didn't even know where Newcastle was, but I had heard they accepted arts students and taught them all the science they needed to become doctors. At the time, I wanted to be a doctor so I could become a Freudian psychoanalyst. To my great shock, they let me in.

In medical school I changed my allegiance from Freud to Oliver Sacks. I planned to be a neurologist and see all the patients who mistook their wives for hats. I knew a few general physicians. To my great shock, they were old guys; they could smell ketones and hear a heart's gallop rhythm from the doorway. I remember one, mid-ward-round, swooping down to pick up a piece of rubbish in the hospital corridor. He held it in front of us and said, "You should take care of the hospital. The hospital is your home." They were old-school dedicated. You know the kind of guys: they hadn't seen their kids for forty-five years. There were not many young general physicians. If anyone had suggested I'd end up doing general and acute medicine, I would have taken it as an insult. By then, you only did that specialty unwillingly – if you didn't get in to *any* other sub-specialty, if your English wasn't too good, or if you wanted to live in the deep bush. General medicine had a bad reputation: it lacked prestige and was considered a dumping ground for the elderly. And who'd want to look after *them*?

By the time of my residency, the old generalists had retired and many general medicine units filled rosters by cutting deals with specialists: *participate in our general medicine roster and we'll give you a 30 per cent infectious diseases appointment.* Other hospitals made do with a "physician of last resort." If you wound up in the emergency department short of breath and with failing kidneys, the renal and respiratory registrars would fight not to take you. The respiratory registrar would say that kidney failure was not a respiratory problem. The renal registrar would say shortness of breath was not a kidney problem. The extremely busy emergency department doctor would ring around, and when everyone rejected you, they'd refer you to the day's rostered physician of last resort – the specialist who for that day was not allowed to say no. Meanwhile, you'd be languishing on an emergency department trolley for ten, twelve, twenty-four hours, waiting to be admitted to a ward. No one was in a hurry; after all, you weren't dying right then, you weren't *crashing* – you were just slowly crumbling.

The House of God is a satirical novel published in 1978 which continues to sell in the tens of thousands. It tells the story of Roy's first year as a doctor in the House of God hospital. There, elderly patients are called "gomers," an acronym for "get out of my emergency room." Throughout a year of sleep deprivation and horror, Roy learns the rules of medicine. Rule number one: *gomers don't die.* Given their immortality and slow recovery, one sure way of getting the gomer off your patient list was to crank their bed up till it hovered six feet off the ground. From that height, the gomer was sure to fall out and break a hip – and then they'd be the orthopaedic team's problem and off your list.

In Australian hospitals, gomers are known as "crumbles" and "acopics" (not coping at home); they are "granny dumps" (popular during holiday seasons), "bed blockers" or "gen med specials." As a registrar, you'd do anything to avoid accepting this kind of patient under your unit's bed card. They had too many problems, were too difficult, probably required family meetings or even a social worker and, worst of all, didn't have problems you could cure. We were all overworked and didn't do medicine to deal with all of that; we did medicine to stick catheters and cameras in people's organs, give drugs that dissolved a patient's problem, perform complex transplants and make it onto the front page of the newspaper.

The House of God is both horror story and black comedy. It paints all the underlying frightfulness of practising medicine, all the unspoken assumptions and prejudices, in full colour. Some medical schools in Australia give copies of this book to their students as a graduation present.

Six years after finishing medical school, the terrible specialist medical exams behind me, and finally about to start my neurology training program, I admitted to myself that despite what Oliver Sacks had led me to believe, *no one* came to a hospital or clinic claiming they'd mistaken their wife for a hat. So I accepted a last-minute job as a trainee in nuclear medicine – interpreting fuzzy scans and injecting radioactive isotopes – but I missed talking with flesh-and-blood patients, regretted leaving the wards. And yet there was no organ system or disease I wanted to dedicate my life to.

My supervisor asked me, "Have you considered general medicine?"

I had not.

"Don't do it!" an endocrinologist friend warned me. "No one will respect you."

Why would caring for a ward full of patients with multiple problems deserve less respect than caring for a ward full of the freshly angiogrammed? I once posed this question to a sub-specialist and he said, "There's less at stake." I asked what he meant. He said, "If you fuck up, it's not such a big deal … so I guess the thinking goes that a lesser physician can do the job."

Half the patients in an acute care hospital are over the age of sixty-five. Study after study has shown that the frail elderly do better in wards dedicated to their care – wards with nurses and doctors and allied health practitioners who know how to care for them. The single most important aspect of care is to have clinicians who *want* to look after this cohort. Generalists, geriatricians, sub-specialists who've crossed to the dark side … it doesn't matter who they are, as long as they have a desire to care for the elderly and feel there is a lot at stake. The frail elderly need clinicians who can look around a ward and see individuals, rather than a mass of castoffs who've somehow snuck into an ivory tower for a bit of inappropriate, grudgingly given treatment.

I am lucky that I work in a well-funded general medical unit staffed by a group of dedicated, full-time general physicians, supported by a tight-knit team of committed nurses and allied health practitioners. I think we are thus able to offer above-average care to our patients, the old and the young. But I have worked in numerous hospitals across three states of Australia and know this to be uncommon. Many general medical units (where they exist) are overstretched, underfunded and caring for far too many patients with a skeleton staff.

One reason aged patients do poorly in hospital is that they become malnourished. They are too weak to eat, too debilitated to negotiate tiny plastic sealed packets of margarine and "fruit salad," and have no one with the time or inclination to feed them. Everyone on every ward in Australia recognises that this is a major problem, but assisting patients to eat is no longer anyone's job. "I didn't go to university for four years to spoon-feed demented patients," I once heard a nurse say. So who does feed our patients? Some hospitals have volunteers, some patients are lucky enough to have families to assist them – many of whom complain that no one is helping their loved one eat, that if they weren't there, they'd starve. And often it's true.

The elderly are inappropriately prescribed far too many drugs. If we follow international treatment guidelines for each disease in the average frail patient on my ward, they receive upwards of twelve drugs a day that need to be taken at five different times of day with the risk of at least ten serious adverse effects. Many elderly patients come to hospital with these kinds of medication regimens. Twenty to thirty per cent of all hospital admissions in those over the age of sixty-five are related to illness directly caused by their prescribed medications. Due to incomprehensible institutional requirements and service fragmentation, upon discharge back to a nursing home, patients have to continue their pre-hospital medications (sometimes the cause of their hospitalisation in the first place) until a GP visits the home, perhaps days later.

All general medical departments are under enormous pressure to treat and discharge patients as soon as possible. They have such a large number of patients that extending each patient's stay by even a single day would cause emergency departments to choke up. However, elderly patients are complex and time is needed to offer them the care they need, to talk to them about their wishes, listen to their experiences of their illnesses, and together forge ways to make their lives bearable. Patients need properly trained nursing staff, quiet rooms with clocks and familiar items, family-friendly visiting hours, assistance with eating, and soothing touch. To do well, patients need to eat, move and remain mentally active in hospital – three things the hospital environment specifically hinders.

HOSPITAL IS NO PLACE FOR THE ELDERLY

Futility

> Our nurses are regularly yelled at by emergency department physicians when they send sick nursing-home patients into hospital, people who can't be treated in the facility, or who wish to attend hospital, or have families who wish them to attend hospital. I wonder what they think a nursing home is, and what a nursing-home resident is. They yell, "Why is this nursing-home resident in my emergency department?" as though a nursing-home resident is like a cockroach or a rat, completely unwanted and unwelcome, undeserving and, most surprisingly, not dead.
>
> – geriatrician, Melbourne

> It's ridiculous: *none* of these patients should be treated. *None* of them.
>
> – surgeon, Melbourne

One solution to the problem of the frail elderly patient in an acute hospital is to try to keep them out. They are viewed as a homogenous and ever-growing group with ever-worsening pathology, demanding ever more hospital beds that no one wants to fund. The media catastrophises, doctors not involved in their care walk through wards and shake their heads, we hear horror stories about some elderly woman admitted to hospital and tortured by the doctors while she sinks to an inevitable death, her body full of puncture holes and draining tubes and externally fixated broken bones. They're on their way out: why can't they – and we – see that?

The argument that the hospital is no place to care for the elderly draws upon several rationales: ethical (the treatment in hospital is ultimately futile, or undermines a person's autonomy); fiscal (we can't afford it); and humanitarian (hospitals precipitate adverse outcomes). The focus on keeping these patients out means we do not make changing our hospitals to meet their needs a high priority.

Much hope for rationing treatment of the elderly is premised on the concept of futility. If the treatment is futile, it shouldn't be offered. The reason the surgeon quoted above declared that all aged, multi-morbid patients should be sent home is that, to his mind, treating them is futile. The resident attending to my grandmother's IV drip was obviously under pressure, overworked and over-tired, but beneath all of that he was filled with a sense of moral righteousness. He was disgusted by the attempt to pump life back into a damaged and dying old body; he couldn't believe someone would choose that, or should even be offered the choice. I recognise the feeling, because I've felt it myself in the past. I'd catch myself – usually towards the end of a long stretch of double shifts – thinking, *What the hell are we doing here?* rather than, *Who is this person? What does he need? What does she want? What can we offer?* The resident's reaction to my grandmother was a failure of empathy, disguised as empathy; it was a failure of imagination. But his righteousness was based rationally on his personal and crystal-clear idea of what was futile.

In offering a patient a treatment, or declining to offer the treatment, it helps to have some idea of whether or not it will work. If we could know with certainty a treatment is futile, our job would be easy. Gone would be much of the worry and sweat, gone the most difficult parts of our conversations about what the patient wants and needs or would like for their life. We'd do what was possible – if the patient wanted it – and no more. The problem is that in all but the most extreme scenarios – the kind of scenarios you read about in the newspaper and I hear about in meetings – futility is almost impossible to define, predict or declare with any certainty.

To suggest that the answer to the question of whether to treat or not should be left to the patient is not a clear way out – reams of data show that doctors can get most patients or their families to agree to any treatment or treatment withdrawal simply by changing the way they present the information. And in Australia it is not solely up to the patient: a doctor is not legally obliged to offer treatment that they deem futile, no matter the patient's or their family's wishes. In fact it is considered unethical to do so. And so medicine has wrangled over the definition of futility. Defining it as a treatment that will produce more burden than benefit seems sound, and yet one must ask: burden for whom? For the patient? Her family? The hospital? The health budget? And who is to decide what burden an individual is prepared to accept for what gain? We should ask the patient, of course, but in order to ask we need to be prepared to offer – and this is the point of contention. Are we prepared to offer a frail elderly patient a hospital stint for a condition from which they will be dead in six months, a year, two years? Deeming something futile when it comes to my cohort of patients is often more moral judgment than data-derived conclusion.

And so we have mined for data to improve the empirical base for our decisions and our conversations with patients – in an attempt to do less harm, to waste less money. We have good data on treatments such as cardiopulmonary resuscitation, and on the survival rates of premature babies and patients with certain diseases. Intensive care units use the APACHE II (Acute Physiology and Chronic Health Evaluation II) score, which estimates the physiological health of an individual, extrapolates from that to information on groups of patients with similar scores, and is applied to individuals as a prognostic tool – giving their percentage chance of surviving intensive care.

But what's a reasonable punt for an individual's life? Should we offer the treatment if there's a 1 per cent chance of survival, based on group data? A 10 per cent chance? Is discharge from hospital to a nursing home a "bad outcome"? And finally, what of the goals of treatment outside raw physiological response, such as offering time for patients and their families to come to terms with imminent death, to grieve, to say goodbye?

*

In one of the hospitals I've worked in over the past thirteen years, I looked after a 92-year-old woman, Pearl, who lived with her (older) sister, Nora. They'd outlived their husbands by decades, and in their sixties moved in together. Pearl had a failing heart, but with medicine and a hospital admission once or twice a year she was able to stay at home: Pearl cooked, Nora cleaned.

The first time I met Pearl was during a short admission for treatment of a urinary tract infection, which had worsened her heart failure. She required antibiotics and some extra diuretics for a few days, after which she felt fine and went home. A few weeks later I walked onto the ward in the morning and saw her name on my unit's list. "She's been palliated," the nurse told me.

I stood at the doorway of her room and watched her lying in the bed in a pink nightie, her eyes closed, her mouth wide open; she was barely breathing. It's very quiet in a single room without drips and blood pressure cuffs and heart rate monitors and oxygen hoses. The sun streamed through the windows onto her bed. But the scene made me anxious. I looked at her and felt no sense of peace, no sense that this was the right thing. I found her notes and pieced together the story.

The ambulance had been called when she became acutely short of breath the evening before. Upon the paramedics' arrival, her oxygen levels were low, so they administered high-flow oxygen on the way to the hospital. When she arrived in the emergency department, she was almost unconscious. A decision was made to palliate. The doctor called Nora and told her that attempts to treat Pearl would be futile. Who'd argue? Certainly not a shocked and terrified 96-year-old woman being told over the phone that her sister was dying. Nora was too distressed even to come in. They moved Pearl to the ward.

I called the respiratory professor and asked if I could run something by him. Wasn't it possible that she'd been given so much oxygen that it depressed her respiratory drive, leading to increased carbon dioxide levels in her blood, which rendered her unconscious? She'd been at home, independent and of completely sound mind. She had a dodgy heart but I thought she deserved a trial of treatment, at the very least. She'd wanted treatment in the recent past. "Who palliated her?" the respiratory professor asked me, then answered his own question: "Probably some young cowboy who saw her age and stopped thinking." He said he'd come straightaway.

We stood by her bedside. Looked at her, looked at each other. He said, "What've we got to lose?"

I knew we had a lot to lose either way, as did the professor. We still didn't know why she'd suddenly deteriorated overnight. Would we cause her distress or harm in our attempt to revive her? If so, we could stop at any time and she would slip away again. But were we robbing her of her chance to go quietly? I knew her, though: remembered how she spoke about her life with her sister. I imagined Nora being called in the middle of the night and told it was all too late. Pearl's sons were on their way from interstate. The worst thing was that she may have been lying there with a slack mouth because of something we had done to her and not attempted to undo.

"Let's give it a go," he said.

He connected an NIV mask, which caused her no discomfort. This mask covers the nose and mouth and pushes air into your lungs – people with obstructive sleep apnoea use similar devices at home each night to maintain their blood oxygen levels. It is not generally considered an invasive or aggressive treatment, and is used in the palliative setting at times to relieve respiratory distress. Its use in Pearl's case was to decrease the carbon dioxide level in her blood – so that if she was unconscious because her levels were too high (as a result of the emergency treatment on the way to hospital), she might regain consciousness.

Eight hours later, she woke up. Her sons had arrived, and brought Nora with them. The family gathered around her bedside. Pearl sat up shakily, sipping a cup of tea and smiling. Her sister clasped my hands. "Thank you," she said. "You're an angel. You're all angels." By then I had tests back that showed Pearl had had a large heart attack. Her prognosis was grim. I told Pearl and her family that I wasn't sure what the next day would bring, that her situation was precarious; we should hope for the best and prepare for the worst. That we would offer full, ward-based treatment and ensure she did not suffer. We agreed that she would be given a trial of NIV treatment again should her breathing deteriorate over the coming days, but that it would be withdrawn if it had no effect or caused her distress.

Pearl slipped into unconsciousness that night and did not respond to the NIV. Her blood pressure dropped, her heart rate slowed. The mask was removed and she slowly stopped breathing.

The treatment we gave her was "futile," and yet for Pearl and her family it was priceless.

*

> I think it could be good to employ psychics in hospital. People always talk about how important it is to "recognise dying," but sometimes it is hard to tell the difference between a dying person and a very sick person who is near death but will be really well if treated appropriately within a few days.
>
> – general physician, Melbourne

Prognostication is an art and a moral judgment, dressed up in a scientific coat. When it comes to the chronic diseases, the best we can do is estimate. The day before they die, a person with advanced heart failure has a life expectancy somewhere between a handful of months and a couple of years. We never know which episode of acute illness will be the last. We can't, therefore, call it all off *just before* the last illness and save all that hospitalisation and cash, because we are never really sure when that will be. We never know – until the person does not get better with treatment, their organs start to shut down and they begin to die.

Futility is not an objective set and we should not pretend that it is when it comes to managing acute illness in the elderly. It includes cultural and institutional expectations, a patient's wishes and values, their physicians' values, and fiscal constraints. We can't simply leave it up to the patient, because they look to us for guidance and prognostic information, for risks and benefits and likelihood ratios. And – most importantly for this group of patients – if an individual doctor decides a certain treatment is futile, there will be no choice for the patient to make at all.

Writing in the *Lancet*, Louise Aronson says:

> Take, for example, a comment made by an otherwise exemplary senior physician at departmental grand rounds after the presentation of a case involving an older man transferred to the hospital from a nursing home. In the middle of a discussion of possible treatment options, this physician remarked that the best solution – the preventive medicine – was never to build nursing homes within 100 miles of hospitals. This quip was greeted with laughter.

Treating a bed-bound, demented patient who has a skin infection with intravenous antibiotics and a trickle of fluid may seem futile to the outsider – but to not treat, to "palliate," will not lead directly to death, just to great pain, gradual ulceration of the skin and perhaps a deep bone infection. This treatment could be administered in a nursing home, in places serviced by visiting hospital teams – but what if there is no visiting hospital team, or the patient becomes agitated and sick in the middle of the night? What if the patient's family would like a hospital doctor to assess their loved one?

Hospitalising and treating an elderly patient for an acute bout of one of their chronic illnesses is rarely outright futile if the patient seeks treatment, if they still wish to try to live. Antibiotics, breathing masks and oxygen, intravenous medicines and fluids are not invasive or torturous treatments that doctors inflict on patients who have called an ambulance in distress. They can be called futile if the patient dies despite these measures, but most of our patients do not die – most of them go home. In the average general medical ward, approximately five patients die out of every hundred admissions. And when they do die, it is generally not something that can be predicted. Much research effort is being directed towards predicting who will die, but I think this research may be misdirected when applied to the elderly with chronic diseases. These patients are complex; they are different from the younger patients with advanced malignancy, for whom such studies have utility. Some of the flurry of research trying to predict who will die before they start dying is fuelled by the researchers' belief that we are over-treating the frail elderly. As such, it is at least in part a scramble to find a scientific basis for a moral belief. But what use will it be to have an app into which I can plug twenty variables and come up with a percentage chance that this episode of breathing difficulty or this episode of dehydration because of too many pills, coupled with a heatwave, will end in my patient's death? We do not know if our treatment was futile until the patient dies. They die: it was futile. They live: we're heroes. Or – perhaps – villains.

We should be honest about our uncertainty. Many palliated patients recover – around 10 per cent. Imagine being told your loved one is dying, only to find them awake and wanting to go home a few days later.

Sustainability

> We had an end-of-life care committee meeting and one nurse went on about how it's all about doctors "not diagnosing dying." Then someone else said, "I really wish we could do something about general medicine and renal – you look at some of these patients and they've had multiple admissions to hospital in the last year, why won't someone just *palliate* them?"
>
> I thought, *what do you think these people have been doing between hospital admissions – lying at home wishing some asshole doctor hadn't treated them?*
>
> – physician, Melbourne

Peter Saul, a medical ethicist and intensive care specialist, writes that, "The truth is dying is not only scary but also scarily expensive. It's widely known that the last year of our lives is when the most health-care dollars are spent … essentially all of this is spent in the last 30 days of someone's life." I often read and hear this statistic. People start their talks by citing this fact; they propose solutions to this alleged problem. It is frequently cited as evidence that doctors are "doing too much" to their elderly patients.

Increasing age and increasing health expenditure go hand in hand, chiefly because there is a greater chance of dying when you are old than when you are young. As people reach their eighties and beyond, their regular use of hospitals and doctors generally declines. So, by some estimates, an ageing population may not break the bank until they start to die in increasing numbers. We spend mostly the same amount – that is, we offer the same degree of care – on each death, young or old, and it is not in fact very much: this suggests that "heroic" efforts to prolong life are actually not commonplace. Data from New South Wales reveals that hospital costs associated with the last year of life actually fall with age, with people aged ninety-five years or over incurring less than half the average costs per person of those who died aged 65–74 years ($7028 versus $17,927). And there has been virtually no change in this pattern over a twenty-year period. We spend the most when people are at their sickest. To save this money, we must all die before we begin to die.

The disastrous scenarios projected as a result of our ageing population are heavily promoted in many quarters, as they support certain ideological beliefs which can then be presented as empirical facts: chief among these facts is that the public medical system is "unsustainable." This is a brilliant word to use to argue the need to slash public spending on health. It is difficult to openly support the unsustainable. And yet "sustainable" is just a word for "what we are willing to pay." Of the world's wealthy nations, Australia spends among the *least* on health as a percentage of GDP – about half that spent by the United States. We have one of the most efficient and effective healthcare systems, and currently have longer life expectancies than most other countries. In fact, according to a recent report issued by the Australian Institute of Health and Welfare (AIHW), our spending on health is currently rising at a far slower rate than at any time since the 1980s. Government funding of health fell in real terms in 2012–13 for the first time in a decade. And per-capita spending on health declined in this period, despite our ageing population. Also, according to another AIHW report, most of the years of life we have gained are healthy years.

The word "unsustainable" is wielded continually by government members and other doomsayers who seek to minimise current financing of a public health system and shift further towards a private, US-style system. Meanwhile, real areas of waste are ignored. Waste such as mass pharmaceutical over-prescription; widespread prescription of heavily promoted, more expensive new drugs; over-servicing of patients in the private sector; and Medicare payments for useless or harmful interventions. All these things need not be addressed if we can blame an ageing population for the need to ration health care – of the aged.

If health-system sustainability – or containment of cost – is an aim, then there is widespread international agreement that we should now be spending more, not less, on integration of care and on prevention. Most of our elderly population live at home and rate their own health as good, often despite various physical limitations. And for the current generation of the elderly there is evidence that people (mostly those from the upper socio-economic strata) are spending more years of their longer lives in good health. If we wish this trend to continue, if we truly wish to address the cost of health care (or the cost of ill health), we should be urgently addressing the poor health of the younger generations. The real tsunami is not one of age per se, but of a population of increasingly poor, obese, diabetic, sedentary young and middle-aged who are the multi-morbid patients of the future and who will require many drugs, doctors, operations (joint replacements, bariatric surgery, amputations, coronary vessel interventions) and hospitalisations.

Good evidence exists about how to reduce the incidence of the non-communicable diseases (including dementia) by attending to six modifiable risk factors: tobacco use, harmful use of alcohol, salt intake, high blood pressure, high blood glucose and obesity. In 2011 the federal government established the Australian National Preventative Health Agency to focus on this task. Following the change of government in 2013, it was defunded in the next year. Medicare Locals, organisations designed to assist GPs to coordinate care, identify gaps at local levels and integrate social and health services, were also largely defunded.

The provision of health care in Australia remains mostly reactive: responding to a crisis, intervening too late, patching a patient up and shipping them off. Most importantly, medical needs and social needs are delivered in a fragmented way by separate organisations. Better integration of GPs and specialists, community services and hospitals has been repeatedly shown internationally to improve a person's health and extend independence. Examples can be found in Denmark, where 24-hour multidisciplinary centres, with GPs and specialists, nurses and allied health practitioners such as physiotherapists and social workers, have been established at the community level. Priority is given to preventing decline, responding early to health problems and supporting citizens to care for themselves and maintain their independence. Relationships are forged, care is individualised, and the need for hospitalisation is reduced.

Public system changes such as these require long-term vision and funding, and in the short term they may not be good for business. What is good for business is to have a population of over-consumers who suffer the health consequences of their over-consumption, which may in turn be addressed by further consumption (of health products), preferably bought in a free market. As we have learnt from watching the American health system turn into a dragon raking gold into its cave, a mostly unregulated fee-for-service private system, where a doctor derives direct financial benefit from doing things to you – and where social supports are sparse – leads to gross over-servicing, massive expenditure and poorer health outcomes.

Over-treatment

The idea that we over-treat people in the last stages of life has gained much traction of late. Articulate and compelling books such as Atul

Gawande's *Being Mortal* paint a picture of medicine gone mad, where doctors routinely torture dying humans. Gawande gives examples such as an intensive care unit full of the almost-dead elderly, who are being kept alive by machines pushed onto them by their specialists.

Ken Murray, a US doctor writing for the *Guardian*, tells us:

> Almost all medical professionals have seen what we call "futile care" being performed on people. That's when doctors bring the cutting edge of technology to bear on a grievously ill person near the end of life. The patient will be cut open, perforated with tubes, hooked up to machines, and assaulted with drugs. All of this occurs in the intensive care unit at a cost of tens of thousands of dollars a day. What it buys is misery we would not inflict on a terrorist. I cannot count the number of times fellow physicians have told me, in words that vary only slightly: "Promise me that if you find me like this you'll kill me."

Also from the US, journalist Jeanne Erdmann offers us the following case history:

> A frail, elderly man lives in a nursing home after a stroke. He can no longer communicate, and his nephews are the only family who speak for him. He ends up in hospital with complications from an infection, then kidney failure sets in. His advance directive specifies no ventilator and no resuscitation following cardiac arrest, but says nothing about dialysis. Yet his nephews feel certain he would not want that treatment and make it known to the kidney doctor, who's pushing for dialysis.

Missing from many of these depictions of medicine-gone-wrong is an analysis of how free-market medicine in the United States has led to such horrific practices. Theirs is a medical system where the relationship between patient and doctor has become a commercial transaction, where an insurance company decides what treatment a patient may or may not have; a system that has led to an erosion of the ethical basis of the patient–doctor relationship. By contrast with the US, in the UK a recent King's Fund review found that the elderly were inappropriately being denied treatments – for heart disease, incontinence, depression and cancer (among other conditions) – that would have improved the length and quality of their lives, because of age. It is widely known and reported in the medical literature that many treatments that would extend and increase quality of life are routinely denied to patients on the basis of their biological age – coronary angioplasty or pacemakers in fit and otherwise well ninety-year-olds, for example. A recent article in the *Lancet* – perhaps the world's most prestigious medical journal – makes the same point: when it comes to the treatment of the elderly, free markets lead to over-treatment, while publicly funded systems risk sometimes unexamined and discriminatory rationing.

No kidney doctor in any Australian hospital I have worked in would offer, let alone push for, a mute nursing-home resident to be given dialysis, nor would any treatment in an intensive care unit likely be offered. For all the talk of patients as consumers with choices they can accept or decline, there are mandated limits to treatment in Australia's public hospitals. Inarguably, the US measures described above are inhumane and unlikely to improve a patient's life. What worries me about the widespread popularity of these tales is that the sentiment from them becomes a blanket philosophy covering all elderly patients in hospital: not just the ones who are dying, not just the ones with cancer and enduring experimental and pointless chemotherapy, but also my frail elderly patients with their dodgy hearts who are still happy to live their lives as best they can. *Medicine is doing too much* becomes the thing to say as you walk through my ward and see all the grey hair against all the white pillow slips.

There is a connection between our horror of ageing while we are young and the rhetoric surrounding excess treatment. On my general medical ward I see no epidemic of excess treatment. A patient calls an ambulance and comes to hospital because they are sick – they may have an exacerbation of their heart disease or lung disease, which has caused them to feel breathless. They may have become incontinent and confused, or fallen because of a urinary tract infection – all of which can be treated quite simply.

Some high-tech intensive care units have extracorporeal membrane oxygenation (ECMO) machines. They function as external lungs for a patient whose lungs are not able to oxygenate their body – for example, if they have severe pneumonia or overwhelming inflammation of the lungs. Patients are given ECMO treatment to support them while their lungs repair – usually for a few days. It was developed in the 1970s to treat premature babies whose lungs were too immature to oxygenate their blood, and is now used for adults as well, typically young adults with severe pneumonia or acute respiratory distress syndrome, who would otherwise die. We don't ever put the elderly on ECMO so they can recover from their pneumonia, although technically we could try. It is not done because ECMO is a precious, hugely expensive technology and survival rates would likely be very low – we don't know how low, because the treatment is simply not offered.

In Australia, patients with severe emphysema are not usually intubated to keep their oxygen levels normal when they get sick, because there is a chance they will never be able to breathe again without the tube in their lungs and because their underlying disease cannot be cured. However, a recent large study in the United States showed that when patients over the age of sixty-five, many with multiple health problems, were intubated for worsening emphysema, over 90 per cent survived. But one intubation would lead to another, and we simply do not have the resources in Australia to intubate someone a few times a year for a chronic condition marked by inexorable decline.

And yet. We do put on life-long home-based ventilation young patients whose spinal cords have been damaged so high up that they are not only quadriplegic but can't move the muscles needed to breathe. We more readily feed, through tubes directly into their stomachs, the young who cannot swallow, and dialyse the young, even when their functional capacity is poor and life expectancy short. I am in no way suggesting that these interventions should be available for all. I am simply trying to illustrate that sometimes the main reason treatments are withheld is that the patient is old and the period of life gained would be shorter than that gained by younger or fitter patients, and as such they do not warrant a portion of the limited resources we have available for these treatments.

Preventable over-treatment does occur in Australia, particularly in the private system. Hundreds of millions of dollars a year could be saved by stopping Medicare funding for treatments that have been proven to have no benefit – such as arthroscopies performed en masse by private orthopaedic surgeons on people with arthritic knees, or expensive "palliative" cancer treatments that may increase some version of life by a few percentage points and inflict manifold misery.

A farmer friend of mine in his sixties needed to renew his heavy-vehicle licence so he could harvest his crop. He saw his GP, who referred him to a private cardiologist for a "check-up." Despite this man being at the peak of health – wiry, physically robust, a regular jogger – with no risk factors for heart disease other than mildly elevated cholesterol, the cardiologist booked him for an angiogram, a procedure that would take the doctor fifteen minutes to perform and make him $2000 to $3000. The specialist told my friend he needed an angiogram to check his coronary arteries, to make sure he wasn't about to have a heart attack: who'd say no? His coronary arteries were completely normal. He went home, got his licence, harvested his crop.

In the private sphere, practitioners often work solo, each discipline practising in isolation. A doctor, once qualified, is free to set up shop wherever they wish and do what they wish to anyone who'll donate their body to the cause. We joke about oncologists driving to church to give a final trial of chemo as their patient's coffin is being carried to its grave. By contrast, in the public hospital cancer treatments are usually debated in multidisciplinary meetings, where surgeons, oncologists, radiation therapists, radiographers and sometimes palliative care specialists are present to discuss the benefits and risks of any particular treatments they may proceed to offer. This collective approach has been rigorously studied and proven to improve all treatment outcomes – including increasing the patient's life expectancy and their quality of life.

Beyond the limits of physiology, the question of rationing is a hugely controversial issue, and politicians, the public and clinicians (except perhaps those dealing with organ transplantation) rarely speak openly about it. We ration all the time and at all levels: government, hospital, ward. The decisions are fraught with difficulties, inconsistencies and discrimination (both rational and corrupt). How much to offer and to whom is dictated by what centralised authorities will fund and by clinical judgment – and then it is an individual and family decision.

In Australian public hospitals, we have not gone the same way as the United States. A general physician I know in Melbourne recently said that he thought we have become unprepared to accept the possibility of poor outcomes for the elderly in medicine, and that this has led to a contraction in treatments being attempted. He asked me, "Faced with death, would you accept a stint in intensive care for a 25 per cent chance of survival and a nursing home as your discharge destination? I would. I'd take those odds." Too bad for him, because it would be a rare ICU that would admit an old patient with those odds.

We ration, we rationalise, and we try to treat rationally. In the end, how far we can go in our public institutions, in what we can offer the sick, is a decision that we make as a society: through our cultural mores and through our acceptance – or not – of the funding limitations imposed upon these institutions by government. For example, when word got out that funding to a lung-transplant program might be cut back, there was uproar from the media and patient support groups. I think, on the whole, the Australian hospitals' rationing of ICU beds and other invasive treatments reflects accurately our community values. Where a family's or patient's wishes fall outside these broad guidelines – such as the request to keep supporting a brain-damaged patient's life on machines they will never live without – a complex series of negotiations take place. This cannot be avoided. The Supreme Court, on the rare occasions it is asked to adjudicate between doctors and families over withdrawal of care, usually supports the clinician's judgment of futility.

We have already limited the treatment options we are prepared to offer the elderly and the frail in Australia. These limitations are mostly sound, however cries for further limitations – based on horror stories from the United States and on cultural winds carrying ideas that treating the elderly is futile or a waste of money – should be opposed. We need to shift our focus to improving that care. It has been limited enough.

My father had a slowly progressive form of leukaemia. In his sixties he was treated with an aggressive form of chemotherapy that slipped into his bone marrow and wiped it out: white blood cells, red blood cells, platelets, everything. When he ran out of platelets, he started to bleed from his nose and his bladder wall. He was hospitalised and hooked up to a catheter that continuously flushed out his bladder so that the flow of urine was not blocked by a clot. He remained cheerful despite terrible nausea, weeping skin infections, a cough and the constant rush of water entering his body.

It was my first year as a doctor. I had only vague ideas about what was going on and no idea of his prognosis. Nothing the doctors tried could stop the bleeding or bring his bone marrow back to life, but they remained cautiously optimistic. He was in there for weeks, yacking to the other pale guy in the next bed, reading the *Herald Sun*, trying to stay hopeful. One night he got up to brush his teeth, slipped and hit his head. "I'm a dickhead," he told the resident who attended to him. "No worries, I'm alright," he said as he was led back to bed. (The resident nervously told me this the next day.) The resident ordered two-hourly neurological observations, so the nurse noticed when overnight my father became unconscious and one of his pupils dilated. When he stopped breathing, he was taken to the intensive care unit and ventilated. The brain scan showed that his skull was full of blood.

At the hospital, my family and I assembled in a side room of the ICU for a meeting with his physician. He summarised, then paused. My family has no medical training. They are not comfortable in hospitals. I asked the questions. No, my father's doctor could not tell us if he would recover. No, he did not know for certain the extent of the brain damage, but it would likely be severe. Then there was the issue of the leukaemia … what, he asked, did we want them to do? Should they switch off the ventilator? My family turned their bewildered faces towards me. I started to cry. The doctor said he'd leave us for a while so we could think about it.

"Try to think about what your father would have wanted," he said.

We all watched our feet. The bone marrow. The horrific flushing catheter. He was so scared of dying, wanted very much to live. My brother wiped his eyes with his fist and said, "He wouldn't want to be retarded."

The doctor came back. I spoke. He nodded. We went to the bedside to say goodbye. My father looked as though he were sleeping, with a tube shoved down his throat. His skin was pink and warm. We stood around him, touched him, hugged him, spoke to his quiet face. Then we stepped out while they switched off the machines and took out the tube. It doesn't take long to look dead. The colour of it, the lack of animation, the cold. The terrible irreversibility.

For years afterwards, I'd wake in the middle of the night gasping for breath, heart pounding, thinking, "What if we decided the wrong thing? What if he'd recovered, after all?" The burden of that decision was immense. Then there were the years I felt it was the right thing to do, but that it was wrong for his doctor to ask us to make the call. My father wanted to live, but he was *dying* – he had intractable bleeding, he had untreatable infections and no bone marrow. I was angry at his doctor for burdening us with the illusion of a decision.

Now I think my pain and anger had nothing to do with the doctor at all, that such reactions were part of my grief. I think it was highly unlikely my father would have recovered, and if he had regained consciousness at all, he would have died soon after from his underlying diseases. Probably the doctor was just offering us time. The situation was enormously distressing for everyone – my father's clinicians, my family. But I do not see how the distress could have been avoided.

*

Hundreds of millions, probably billions, are being spent for little value to the patient. That money could go both elsewhere in the health system and to reduce its budgetary impact. Not just in general surgery but in intensive care we need to think carefully about what we do to ageing Australians … Far better we make these decisions ourselves when we are fit and well and rational. We can do this by making what is called an Advance Medical Directive. A senior medical professional recently strongly urged them to be mandatory for everyone over 73. He says if you don't do it then you shouldn't have a Medicare card. I am not sure how we can make people do this but I am sure we have to find a way.

— Amanda Vanstone, the *Age*, April 2014

Fred was an 84-year-old man who came to hospital short of breath and feeling weak. He had a history of quite severe heart failure but still managed at home independently. The registrar who admitted him overnight suspected influenza, so Fred was sent to an isolation room and we had to don gloves, masks and gowns before we could talk to him. We did our stuff — took a history, examined him — he had fluid overload and a badly infected ear. I explained that the treatment was antibiotics and fluid-removing medicine in his vein. He nodded. I turned to leave, then looked back at him. He looked utterly miserable.

I sat down on his bed, covered from head to toe in protective gear, and asked how he was going at home, what he did. He told me he worked as a lollypop man and had recently had his driving restricted to ten kilometres around his house. I expressed admiration at the former, sympathy for the latter. He looked at me for a long time, then started talking nonstop: he told me he wanted to die, that he didn't want to come to hospital, that his GP had called the ambulance. "I hate hospital, hate it," he said. He told me his wife had had dementia and had been in care for many years and that he'd visited her every day. That she'd died last year. That they'd both believed in euthanasia and if only it was legal, he'd be gone. He told me his dog had died six weeks ago and that she'd been all he had left in the world. He was sobbing. "I don't want to be here. My GP made me come," he said. "I'm just a nuisance, a nuisance to everyone."

I told him he was not a nuisance, that we were happy to care for him and that he'd probably feel better with treatment, but that he didn't have to come to hospital if he didn't want to. That we could try to arrange treatment in his home, and that if he got worse he could go to the hospice. He said, "I believe in euthanasia. Why can't we just do that? They put my dog down, they put my little dog down." I said, "You are unwell and I don't think we should make a decision just now, but I'll come back later and we'll talk again." I didn't think he had influenza, so we took him out of isolation.

Later in the day I went back to see him. He said, "I've thought about what you said, doc, and I want to go to the hospice. I want to. I want to die." I told him I didn't think he was dying, so he couldn't go to hospice just then, but that we could make plans for the future if he didn't want to come to hospital again. And then we talked for over an hour: about his dog, his wife and his family, and how he'd visited his wife's mother and then his wife every day they were in nursing homes, and what he planned to do for Christmas and his job, and how he had once been a hospital volunteer. He kept saying he was a nuisance to everyone now; how he couldn't get to his favourite river to fish for cod because he was not allowed to drive that far; and how wonderful his marriage was, and his dog, and now they were both gone and he had no one.

I didn't know what to say. He looked at me, his cheeks wet, waiting for me to say something. I said his wife and dog were lucky to have had him, and that he was evidently a man who was full of love and the world needed that – there's not nearly enough of it. He was not a nuisance; on the contrary, he had a big contribution to make. I asked him if he'd thought about getting a new dog. He said he was scared to get a new dog because it would be unfair to the dog when he died, that it would be sent to the pound and put down. We talked frankly about his prognosis: months to a few years. He mulled that over for a minute or two.

I said, "I'm pretty sure we can arrange for someone to adopt your dog when you die."

He looked down. "Let me think about it," he said.

The next morning he was sitting up, dressed, and he opened his wallet to show me pictures of his old dog. His breathing had improved a little; he smiled for the first time. We talked about rivers within ten kilometres of his house – there was one, but it was filled with "rotten carp."

"Good," I said. "Get out there and kill them."

He improved and was discharged home with an arrangement to participate in weekly physical rehabilitation and have contact with a card group, as he'd been a card shark in years past. A nurse whose daughter had wanted "eighty-eight puppies" for Christmas volunteered to be the dog carer should anything happen to Fred.

I called him two weeks after he arrived home to see how he was and to discuss with him his wish not to come back to hospital. He was exuberant on the phone. A dog breeder had given him a retired show dog under the proviso that should Fred ever become unable to care for her, it would be returned to them. "Can you believe that?" he said. "The one thing I was worried about, and they wanted that too!"

I said, "Fred, you told me you didn't ever want to come back to hospital."

He said, "Of course I want to come back if I get sick. I get silly when I'm sick. I hate everything. I say silly things."

His GP probably knew that, which was why he sent him in.

*

Almost every day an elderly patient will tell me – with shame – that they are a burden or a nuisance, that they're taking up a hospital bed someone else needs. They apologise for being a pain, a drain, for wasting my valuable time, for being sick and needing help. I always tell them: "We want to look after you. This is your bed. You paid your taxes your whole life, didn't you? Well, then, here's where you claim your benefits."

Hospitals have begun to set up annex clinics where patients are assisted by a trained stranger to draw up a list of treatment limitations, based on future hypothetical situations. In some states and territories, these documents are legally binding. Directives and written plans are promoted as being a support to patient autonomy, a way to enable a person to be in control of their health care and their death. Some hospitals have developed programs where teams of planners operate autonomously in the hospital. These programs were developed in the United States, sold like franchises and are often championed by intensive care doctors – doctors who usually see patients at their worst, who rarely have relationships with them, and who may believe trenchantly that we are over-treating the elderly. These doctors are never there on the days when the majority of our patients are sitting on the sides of their beds, fully dressed, their overnight bags packed and their walking sticks at the ready. In the roving planners programs, any member of staff can call the planners and request that they see a patient. A nurse on night shift, a physiotherapist, someone walking past the patient who thinks they might benefit from a talk about what they don't want, anyone who thinks the patient should be offered a chance to die – all can ask for the patient to be seen, to be offered a choice. Without the involvement of the treating clinician.

A readiness to not-treat at the slightest sign may have unintended and adverse consequences, particularly for those who are vulnerable due to loneliness and a conviction that they are burdensome. What does it mean to "respect patient choices"? It would have been easy to take what Fred said at face value and respect his "wish to die," rather than to help him edge out of an extended grief state, help him find value in his life, help him have hope and a future that could be bearable. But marking his chart "for palliative care only" or putting in place an advanced care directive that he not be admitted to hospital again would have been doing worse than nothing.

*

I walk with a distinctive heavy footfall and wear heels that tend to rap. The first time I walked into David's room, he smiled and said, "With a stomp like that, you must be the boss lady." He was in his early eighties, lived at home with his wife and had mild dementia. He'd come to hospital for treatment of a chest infection. At the front of his file was a photocopy of his plan, dated two weeks ago and filled out at an advanced care planning clinic.

"You have an advanced care plan," I said.

"Yes!" his much younger wife snapped.

"A what?" he said.

"A plan stating what you do and don't want me to do." I held it in front of him. "Do you remember filling this out?"

He peered at it. "No."

His wife laughed nervously. "You remember, David." She turned to me. "He remembers. It's his wishes."

I said to David, "It says you like Lester Young."

"I love Lester Young."

We laughed.

I read the plan. The wish not to be a burden featured prominently.

The next day, I was in the corridor, walking towards his room, and a few steps away from the doorway I heard him call out, "Here she comes!"

So his memory wasn't that bad.

Every time I saw him, this man filled with wit and life, I wondered who had wanted the advanced plan. Who was scared of being burdened?

I feel great sympathy for David's wife, as it is likely that David will increasingly become what could easily be described as a burden: he will require her care and assistance, necessitating a curtailment of her leisure and an increase in her labour. I feel this sympathy alongside a desire to protect my patient from experiencing the guilt of knowing he may be a burden. It is not a trivial thing to feel you are harming your loved ones. That our elderly often feel that their dependent existence causes difficulties for their family is both a reality and a tragedy. But I think of my daughters and know I would do anything to prevent them suffering unnecessarily; I would hate to be a burden to them.

Joan Didion writes:

> No one wants to be a "burden." Few of us want to be perceived as considering our own lives more important than the ongoing life and prosperity of the family. Few of us will sit with a husband or wife or child in a lawyer's office or a doctor's office and hesitate to sign the piece of paper that will mean, when the day goes downhill, the least trouble for all concerned. For all the emphasis on the importance of "choice," the only choice generally approved by the culture is to sign the piece of paper, "not be a burden," die.

We can never untangle entirely the complex web of motivations and considerations behind end-of-life decisions. And what should we consider a sound motivation? Many elderly people fear that they are or will become an encumbrance to their loved ones; they quite reasonably seek to prevent this, and it explicitly informs many end-of-life decisions. A clinician's task is to ensure we do not intensify the patient's feeling that they are a burden – we must be cognisant of it and attempt to alleviate it: take the person in, let them know we can carry them. When placing limits on treatment, it is sometimes far from clear whose distress we are seeking to curtail.

We are all of us irrational, divided, opaque and oblique creatures. We communicate in a multitude of ways: with our eyes and hands and bodies and heart rate, as well as with words we may or may not mean. We may ask for – think we want – the opposite of what we wish for. We change our minds. This is what it is to be human. All of which poses a large problem for the patient-choice movement in medicine in its more simplistic manifestations.

*

I once cared for a patient named George who was in his eighties and had recently moved into a nursing home. He was brought in to hospital with an infection and confusion, and was incidentally found to have a very slow heart rate. His infection was simply treated, his confusion would likely resolve, but he needed a pacemaker or he would probably die. The cardiologists said they would insert the pacemaker if I thought it was warranted, if he was for active treatment. In truth, the question surprised me – why should he not receive a pacemaker? He wasn't terminal and didn't have severe dementia or advanced metastatic cancer. His illness was completely treatable. His life expectancy was good. All that was against him was mild cognitive impairment and the fact he lived in a nursing home.

I organised a family meeting and discussed the situation with his daughter – who would need to consent to the procedure – and her husband. Her husband told me that George had been depressed since moving to the nursing home, and had often told him that he wished he were dead. "He spends most of the time in his room, lying on the bed. He'd be happier to just go. We should just let him go." I asked what his daughter thought. She told me that George had several lady-friends when he was still living at home. She raised her eyebrows twice, "*Several* lady-friends." I asked her what her sense of her father's life was now. She kept looking from her husband to me. "I don't know," she said. "He's never said to me that he wanted to die. He's been tired and it's definitely been hard for him to lose his house …" The husband and wife debated whether he would want a pacemaker or not: whether he would want to live or not. I expressed sympathy for George's situation, and mentioned that the transition to residential care was often a difficult one, that it could take him time to adjust. I told her that there was every possibility his slow heart rate had caused his fatigue, and that he might feel better with a pacemaker.

His daughter said, "I went to the facility today to pick up some of his things and all the women in the dining room were asking: 'When's George coming back? Is he okay? Give him our best. Tell him we're waiting for him.'" She laughed, shook her head: "Always the ladies."

I rang the cardiologist and told him the daughter was happy for him to go ahead. "Good," he said. "That's what I thought we should do too."

It has become easy to not-treat, to palliate. This is not necessarily a bad thing, but there is more than patient choice and the avoidance of futility at play in this shift. And there are risks that accompany it.

I spoke with Professor Paul Komesaroff about his end-of-life discussions with his mother, a frail elderly woman with advancing dementia, whom he cared for. He said:

> My mother had been a very strong advocate of euthanasia and had entrusted me with an enduring power of attorney twenty-five years ago on the basis that she did not ever want to live in a dependent state. In spite of that, as her horizons shrank, so did her expectations and goals. Even though I reminded her of her commitment to euthanasia and to avoiding living in a state that didn't meet her goals or expectations, she was adamant that she found her life satisfying and rewarding. She would respond to me with incredulity when I said, "Remember how you used to talk about euthanasia?" and she would say, "Well, I don't want to die. Why are you even raising the question?"
>
> And then at one stage she announced to me that the time for her to die really had arrived, that she was no longer able to make a contribution to other people's lives – that was how she put it. Over the weeks that followed she made it clear that she had reached a point where she was satisfied that she had achieved a state of fullness, and she was now prepared, at last, to allow her life to come to a close should she become ill.

These decisions often occur in dialogues; they are mutual acts of interpretation. Decisions made as a well seventy-year-old may not reflect one's wishes as a ninety-year-old with many physical and mental impairments. Those impairments may turn out to be bearable, after all. People change their minds. Studies show that people's desire for future hospital treatment is lowest soon after a period of hospitalisation. As the months go on, they become more likely to want that treatment again in the event of deterioration; they "get back on the horse," so to speak. This makes sense and is why patients who do eventually decline treatment or hospitalisation have often been hospitalised several times in quick succession – with each hospitalisation bringing a shorter period of improvement. They get tired and are no longer prepared to carry the burden of treatment for such small benefits. Booking someone into an advanced care planning clinic to document their wishes directly after hospitalisation – the time they will be most likely to state they do not want hospital treatment ever again – may inappropriately deprive a patient of future hospital care, or inappropriately mark them for palliation. Should they arrive by ambulance six months later in a state which makes it impossible for us to communicate with them – too short of breath, too confused, in too much pain – we will read their plan and see they do not want treatment, and we will not necessarily seek out the cause of their problem (which in all of the above scenarios might be something simple and simply treatable). We will start the morphine and midazolam infusion, as this is what they said they wanted. Who's to know if they changed their mind three months after writing the plan? If life's not so bad right now and they'd appreciate an antibiotic or a trickle of oxygen, a bed for a few days and a week in rehab?

If someone had asked my grandmother even six months before she became house-bound and oxygen-dependent if she would rather die than be in that state, she would have said yes, and yet her gradual decline remained tolerable to her; she found that she still wanted to live.

Thomas Nagel writes:

> Suppose, for example, that you sign a directive asking to be euthanised, or allowed to die of a treatable infection like pneumonia, if you should reach a condition of advanced dementia in which you don't remember anything and can't recognise anyone. It is possible to be in such a condition without intolerable suffering, and even to enjoy eating peanut butter and jelly sandwiches. Does autonomy really give your past self the authority to kill off this later self?

Why would a tertiary institution want to offer an advanced care planning service? Many of the people directing and working in these services are well-intentioned and feel strongly that they are responding to an urgent need. It is true that doctors may not always – or at all times – have the wherewithal to explore sensitively a patient's wishes. But farming this job out to someone who is not involved with the patient's care and has no sanction to intervene in their life circumstances is not the solution.

Professor Nicholas Talley, the current president of the Royal Australasian College of Physicians, writes, "The promotion of advance care planning as part of better end of life care management is just one of the many ways that physicians [specialists] could play a critical role in 'future-proofing' healthcare spending." There is often in the advocacy for these plans a whiff of resource-saving, of a belief that "probably billions" are being wasted on the elderly. As such, there is a danger that we are not offering a real choice – even if we believe we are – but merely securing acquiescence. I asked a woman who works in one of these clinics interstate if the documents – signed, sealed and delivered to a patient's electronic medical record – are ever reviewed. She looked confused and said, "I guess they could be, if the patient requested it." Had she ever seen a patient more than once? She had not.

Perhaps this movement will prove transitory. In January 2015 the Victorian department of health sent out a memo to all hospitals, stating, "The department does not support the establishment of stand-alone advance care planning clinics. Health services are reminded of their obligation to provide tertiary and secondary care and not to substitute for primary [GP] care."

Written treatment plans have a place: where people have a strong and sustained wish to avoid particular treatments or interventions that might be offered to them in the future. However, requiring the entire aged population to have such documents is not in their best interests. All we can hope for is that people with an advanced illness have ongoing discussions with their doctor or family or enduring power of attorney about their changing goals and values, so that these may be taken into account when treatment decisions arise. Mandating anything more defined than that is forcing us to place bets before we even know what kind of race we're betting on. If we as a society want to have a national electronic system where limits on care are documented, legally binding and immutable, it should also be mandated that they be reviewed regularly. A monthly review does not seem too taxing, given that it is your life you would be registering. We register our cars – those non-sentient hunks of metal – yearly.

Both my mother and her sister ended up with a long stretch of perfectly lucid and pain-free, though meaningless and purposeless, days. They found that unbearable. They could not abide struggling each day to distract or amuse themselves – to somehow fill the unending string of days. This long stretch of purposeless days may well have cost my mother her religion. My aunt didn't even have a terminal illness and that compounded her problem. For both of these women, life is simply not about trying to keep yourself amused, much less comfortable. Both of these women felt stuck, though my aunt found a way out by not eating, and she was fortunate enough to be in a nursing home that supported her decision.

– Professor John Hardwig, University of Tennessee

Last week, I performed a short local anaesthetic procedure on a woman in her nineties who was in the late stages of dementia. She was accompanied by an employee from her nursing home, and also by her husband. My patient seemed catatonic, didn't seem to notice the pain of the local anaesthetic. She was not able to communicate with me in any way as I operated on her. What was the point in this? I thought. Why was I performing surgery on a person who clearly had no quality of life and would probably soon die? As I wrote my op note, I looked up at her husband and, in a knowing way, said to him, "It must be awful for you." I was thinking of assisted dying, how his wife was the embodiment of why it should be available. With bright eyes and a completely steady voice he responded. "Oh no, dear, not at all! I go and visit her every day. And, when we are alone, she knows exactly who I am. And we hold hands and we share things. We still love each other, you see."

– Gabriel Weston, surgeon

When I was in medical school, my mother visited my great-aunt Mickey —
who had severe dementia — in her nursing home every week. She would
wash and set her hair, read to her, bring her food. Every now and then
she'd call and invite me to join her, and tell me stories of all the small
indignities Mickey suffered there: her toenails left so long they'd curled
round and cut into her flesh; the faeces on her dressing gown; grime in
the creases of her skin. I'd get angry as she talked: not at the neglect, but
at the fact my mother insisted on telling me about it. I didn't want to
know.

"I don't know why you bother," I'd say.

"It makes her so happy," my mother would counter.

"Don't you *realise?*" I once said. "She doesn't even know who you are."

"But I know who she is," my mother said.

*

The first time I see Irena, we are two doctors down and have a full waiting room. I call her name, four times. Finally she stands up: ninety-four
years old, 125 centimetres tall.

The clinic is for elderly patients with multiple chronic problems: failing
heart, kidneys and lungs, dissolving bones and aching joints, bone marrow that's drying up. There is a desk between us, and I am supposed to
type notes directly into the computer as they talk, as if I am a travel agent.

Though deaf, Irena whispers. I look at her: cataract, arthritis, stains on
her cardigan, false teeth that are too big for her gums so they move up
and down independently of her lips when she speaks. I leave the desk and
sit next to her so I can hear. Her English is halting, slow as calligraphy. I
ask her if next time she wants me to arrange a Russian interpreter. She
looks at me and raises an eyebrow: "You don't like my English?" I ask her
how she has been since she last came to the clinic. She says what she says
every time thereafter: "I am ninety-four, doctor. I am old." She always
pauses here and raises a finger before delivering her punchline: "But I am
not dead yet." Then she laughs.

I sit beside her to feel her pulse or listen to her lungs, and she tells me snippets that over months become grand narratives. In Stalin's Russia, her husband was taken to a labour camp for running his own business as a tailor. They wouldn't let him take his violin. For a year, this tiny woman travelled to the camp every week and demanded they give it to him. She wrote letters. To Stalin. They relented. Her husband played so beautifully he was granted an unofficial reward: though it was against the rules, Irena could stay with him in the camp for a week.

Once patients enter a nursing home, they are no longer eligible to attend this clinic. It's another world, and all the rules change. I know Irena is on her way there when I sit next to her doing something clinical and she whispers in her ancient staccato, "Doctor. This week. I dirtied myself. Two times."

After Irena misses two appointments in a row, I find out she's been moved to a home. I am sad and increasingly troubled by questions about the camp that only she can answer. Did her husband have his own room? What was in it? Was there a window? Was the bed comfortable? What did they eat? Was she happy? I start to feel panicked when I think of her. What was it like in there?

I call the nursing home and ask them to ask Irena if I might visit. She says to come tomorrow.

Irena's room has a narrow bed, a wardrobe, a bar fridge and a single armchair. I sit on her walking frame and ask how she is. She is old, but not dead yet. We laugh at this. She tells me she fell and thought she was being taken to hospital but instead found herself in this room. Someone brings one cup of tea and a dark brown biscuit and smiles at me over Irena's head. Irena dips her finger into the plastic cup, says, "Cold," and pushes it away. When I stand up to leave, she opens her fridge. It is full of brown biscuits, piled into the door shelves and drawers. She insists that I take some and wraps a handful in a napkin. She puts the parcel in my hands: "Will you come again?"

No one wants to go to a nursing home. My patients fear it; families often feel terrible guilt when the time comes: it is thought of as an abandonment. Nursing homes are where we place our bad outcomes, our frail, our no-longer-independents. They are places people go to wait safely to die. The old doubly incontinents. You might have stood up to Stalin, you might still read Tolstoy, but if you're losing it from both the front and the back and you're not a two-year-old, you're going to be hidden away.

"Don't knock the nursing homes, they do a pretty good job," a geriatrician said to me. And most of the time they perform their function: as a holding bay for old people. Most of the time.

Not so long ago I cared for a bed-bound woman with dementia named Iris. She was sent into hospital after a new GP visited her nursing home. The home was originally designed to care for semi-independent people and had been de-regulated (as all homes in Australia are now) to accommodate residents requiring more intensive "high-level" care. Iris was mute and grossly wasted and in no distress, but under her nightie she had bedsores so extensive and deep that I could see her hipbones and sacrum – the bones, the ligaments and thin strands of the little muscle she had left. The sores were ten centimetres wide and red-raw. The nurse was standing by her bed spooning porridge into Iris's open mouth. She stretched her neck out like a baby bird, waited eagerly for the next mouthful: she was starving.

A starved and neglected resident at a care facility is a rarity in Australia; inspections are frequent, attention to basic needs is usually adequate. Their human needs are another story.

About a quarter of Australians over the age of eighty-five now live in care facilities. Dementia is the reason half of them have been institutionalised. In Australia people currently live an average of three years once placed in residential care. Residents go outside for an average of ninety-six seconds a day. Studies show that constant and severe loneliness is reported by up to 50 per cent of residents. Staff attitudes towards residents vary from caring to dismissive. Ageism is rife and largely accepted – by staff as well as residents and their families. Residents are often told when they may eat, drink, wash, toilet and go outside. False assumptions are made about what a person is capable of doing or might like to do. Josh Planos, writing in the *Atlantic* about his grandmother, commented, "She spent her last days in a nondescript building where doctors told her what she wasn't, rather than what she was."

Many studies have shown that in the face of isolation and lack of responsibility, people with dementia deteriorate more swiftly. The so-called behavioural-and-psychological symptoms of dementia (aggression, agitation, hallucinations) are intensified by lack of familiar faces and a lack of mental stimulation or meaningful work. Intractable and severe symptoms are rare, suffered by less than 1 per cent of people with dementia. Mild symptoms can be prevented or ameliorated by attention to a person's human needs. But it is far more expensive and complex to attend to these human needs than it is to administer sedating drugs.

Nurses working in care facilities are paid the least of all nurses. Currently, their average age is fifty and there is a major shortage of new recruits. Personal care assistants, who often have only a few weeks of training, fill the gaps. Who'd choose to enter a specialty that is lowest in the hierarchy in every sense? More importantly, why does caring for the elderly sit low in hierarchies? Hierarchies of what?

Programs have been developed in an attempt to humanise these institutions: gardens established, chickens and other pets supplied, outings and upgrades (you can pay extra and get in-house haircuts and chilled white wine). But they rarely address the lack of responsibility and autonomy, or the isolation of many of our elderly citizens housed in these poor, fair or exemplary places. People do not need distractions and entertainments to lead a good life – they need meaning: love and work.

There are facilities that have made offering holistic, humane and individualised care a priority. But this is the exception rather than the norm. Again, institutions and staff reflect the wider culture.

I watched a documentary about nursing homes and one clip showed a carer sitting with a bed-bound and mute resident. On camera the resident appears to be in a minimally conscious state. The carer sits close, her hands on his hands, his forearms, stroking his face. She says, "I'd go home thinking of what it would be like to be in this position, and [I thought] what he would be missing was probably human touch … we do have a special language, a special way of communicating, just not through words … it's through human touch. It's just one human relating to another human." I found watching this profoundly moving. I feel sure it must have been a great comfort to the man, as touch is to any person, from the moment they unthinkingly wail out of their mother's body into the world. She had obviously grown to love this man and so was treating him with the greatest of care. How many unvisited nursing-home residents feel love?

There is a nursing home on the outskirts of Amsterdam that features frequently in the press and is held up as a stellar example of innovative care. De Hogeweyk is a gated, fake village that houses 152 residents with dementia. Nursing assistants staff "stores" and "cafés," and the entire property is under video surveillance. There is a town square, gardens and a cinema. That this is a vast improvement on the sterile hospital environment of a standard nursing home is undeniable, and yet there is something creepy about the notion that we need to construct alternate universes – *Truman Show* theme parks – to contain the elderly.

*

Min ran an inner-city boarding house for students from the 1950s till the late 1990s. She lived next door, and the two houses shared a backyard. She was generous, cared for the students, and collected bottles and donated the money to Yooralla. Michael Cathcart, now an ABC radio broadcaster and historian, lived in the boarding house in the 1980s for ten years while he was a student at Melbourne University. He describes Min as a spry and sharp lover of company and beer – she was usually cheerfully tipsy by 4 p.m. She was well known to the local community, visited Victoria Market a few times a week to buy her meat and vegetables from store-holders who'd known her for decades, drank at the local pub. In her late eighties, Min's health and mental state started gradually to decline. Instead of her caring for the students, they started to care for her; in particular, Michael — then writing his PhD — and his friend and fellow boarder Victor took on this role. After Min fell and fractured her hip, she was sent for a stint in rehab and then back home. Social workers intermittently visited the house. Min failed their cognitive tests and mixed up words — would ask for her bone, rather than her stick — but those in the house understood her.

"She's drinking *beer*! Have you seen the meat in her fridge? She's in there *boiling a cantaloupe*!" the social workers would cry.

"What does it matter?" Michael said when they told him she was at risk and needed to be placed in a nursing home. "Ninety-two is a risky thing to be. This is how she wants to live."

Min's care needs grew more intense; she became incontinent. Michael and Victor found themselves drawn into her more intimate care. They would get her out of bed in the morning and clean her up, and she'd follow the same routine as she had for decades: collect bottles; visit the pub, her solicitor and the market; come home with food and eat it. She became increasingly unsteady on her feet, so the pub started serving her sarsaparilla, rather than beer. The store-holders at the market understood what she wanted and gave her the right change. She was propped up by a close-knit community. Michael says, "She'd lost vocabulary, was physically frail, but had the spirit of a hero." She wanted desperately to stay at home, and the community rallied around her to enable it.

Suspicious about what the students' motives might be in caring for their landlady, the social workers arranged for a hearing at the public advocate. Min's solicitor was appointed her guardian and she was allowed to return home. Finally, a nurse was engaged to visit each morning and attend to her rising, washing and dressing. Michael says he took care of her because he had grown to love her and felt the house owed her a debt, given she had looked after so many of its residents. However, he acknowledges that if, at the start of his involvement, someone had outlined the amount of care he would eventually be giving Min, he would have deemed it unmanageable. The increasing support he and Victor provided was incremental, so gradual that they just accepted the changes as necessary and natural.

*

Many families care for their ageing loved ones, to varying degrees. Caring and being cared for are mutually enriching experiences. They give purpose and meaning to the lives of both giver and receiver. However, while it may be a precious period of life together, it can also be very difficult, emotionally and physically. And there is a dearth of social supports available to make it less onerous. When an old person receives support from someone who is not related (often a neighbour), we tend to view it with suspicion: what is the helper getting out of this?

Japan has a population with the largest proportion of elderly citizens in the world. Traditionally, the frail elderly were cared for by their families, but as in all developed nations, geographical separation or full-time work made this increasingly difficult. Starting in the 1980s, hundreds of grassroots volunteer programs were established to fill gaps in the skeletal services provided by government. These programs grew and coalesced in 1992 into a movement known as *Fureai kippu* ("caring relationship tickets"), where individuals earn health-care credits by supporting an elderly person in their neighbourhood. Credits may be spent on their own family's care needs or saved for future personal use. Then, in 2000, Japan instituted a major overhaul to ensure universal access to quality, intensive, individualised aged care. A long-term care insurance scheme was introduced, funded equally from government revenue and compulsory payments by all citizens over the age of forty. The scheme finances integrated health and social care, access to round-the-clock home care, nursing visits, dementia-specific day centres, group homes, respite care and rehabilitation. Only 2.8 per cent of Japan's aged currently reside in nursing homes.

Countries across Europe are now seeking to transform attitudes to people with dementia: funding large media campaigns that challenge negative assumptions, linking young with old, funding day-care programs (including small groups hosted in people's homes one day each week), training businesses to attend to customers with cognitive impairment, educating schoolchildren, finding ways to include those with dementia in society.

A number of regional cities in Australia have also made efforts to become dementia-friendly, changing public services and educating residents of the town to support those with dementia to participate in their communities and remain at home despite their impediments. Is it possible for us to make this the norm? It seems barely imaginable, and would require a large shift in social and institutional values and structures. Public seating and toilets, smooth footpaths and slow traffic have all been shown to help. There have been calls to construct supported accommodation for those needing care within bustling cities, to reduce isolation and enable integration with a community.

We see in these places a shift in perspective: the elderly are not a growing cost to be managed or a burden to be shifted or a horror to be hidden away, but people whose needs require us to change our society. They are those for whom we are responsible and to whom we owe real care – in the form of both time and funds.

A change in training and legislation is urgently needed to address the state of care in all nursing homes. If it can be done well in some places, it can be done well across the board. Ensuring hygiene and safety is not enough. We would be outraged if a child-care centre sat its charges in a room in front of a television for ten hours a day. Even in the later stages of dementia, people remain capable of challenge, engagement, creativity and love.

Hospitals and nursing homes are not shops, or hotels; they are precious public institutions; they are ours. They need help if they are to become more humane: help to drive patients home, keep them company, walk them to the café, assist patients to eat, provide books and magazines, radios and conversations. Public institutions can't hire someone to talk to each patient for a couple of hours a day even if it does prevent delirium and deterioration; at present they barely have the funds to provide basic care. And perhaps such acts are better for both giver and receiver if they arise from the community, rather than an institution.

If we are to welcome the elderly into our communities and support them to stay there for as long as possible, if we are to attend to the social needs of our elderly citizens both inside and out of institutions, then we need both government intervention and funding, along with the community's engagement and help.

My grandmother got better in hospital and came home to my parents' house. She was happy with her ever-shrinking life. She couldn't use the portable oxygen cylinders to get herself to the shops anymore, and she had a lot of pain from her breaking bones. But she was mostly independent with her "activities of daily living," as showering, toileting, cooking and cleaning are known in hospital.

"What do you do all day?" I asked her.

"I remember," she said, holding up her finger and smiling mightily. "I have so many memories to play with."

She read the paper and ate dinner with her family; she was happy to be alive.

But slowly her breathing deteriorated, her fingers turned purple and then she couldn't get out of bed. Slowly, she reached the point when she couldn't think about anything except her next breath, and it was never quite enough. My parents both worked full-time, I was away at university, there was no one to help her to the toilet, and the bones in her spine were collapsing, having been weakened by the little white tablets she'd been prescribed by her physician.

She and I talked about what to do. I suggested the hospice. She agreed. I called her doctor and the palliative care service. The person I spoke to at the hospice – I do not recall if it was a nurse or a member of the administrative staff – said, "Pulmonary fibrosis? They tend to linger …" I begged her. I was always begging. Begging or flinching or holding my breath. Eventually they arranged for Nan to be admitted to the hospice, where she was given drugs to relieve the torture of slowly drowning, drugs to relieve her pain. Where the nurses gently tended to her personal physical needs – bathing and toileting, eating when she was hungry, drinking when she was thirsty, sucking on moistened swabs when she could no longer swallow.

I visited her every day. The ward was a peaceful and kind place. I'd bring a book and climb into bed with her. She'd rest her head on my shoulder and close her eyes. Even when she couldn't talk, she would smile when I lay in her bed and held her.

All my family kept asking me, "When is Nan going to die?"

It began to rain: unusual, tropical rain. The kind of rain you thought might burst the hospital windows. The kind of rain that would have made Nan's eyes glitter in happiness for the long drink it offered her trees. It rained for days. First, she failed to notice the rain. Then she stopped talking altogether. Then she no longer opened her eyes for more than a flicker. Then, on the twelfth of November, her breaths grew light and slow and sickly sweet. Then, while I held her small body in my arms, she drew a long breath in and out and she just stopped. Her eyelids flew open and her blue eyes bulged out as if she was shocked at some terrible news. And then I can't tell you how still she became.

I have had people shake their heads when I tell them she died in a hospice. "What a pity," they say. "She should have died at home." In survey after survey, the vast majority of adults in Australia state that they wish to die at home. Only 14 per cent of people in Australia die at home: half die in hospital, 30 per cent in nursing homes. More people in America – within that healthcare system of horror – die at home than in Australia. This is often cited as a failure of our system; I think that is a myth.

If I try to imagine dying right now, I too prefer to imagine myself at home, in my own bed, having just sipped from my favourite teacup, the lighting just right, my family all around me. A general physician from Melbourne told me, "People tend to believe in a Hollywood death, where there's no preamble, you're clean and cool with your head resting on a crisp pillow, and you slowly close your eyes, turn your head and fall asleep forever." This is not a common type of death.

In the 1950s my grandmother's husband developed a brain tumour. They knew it was a brain tumour because he was fixing his car one day and his right arm rose straight above his head all by itself. Nan said they both stood there by the car, staring at his risen arm as if it were an intruder. Eventually he was unable to get out of bed and my grandmother cared for him at home. The doctor – she told me – taught her how to inject morphine. Her eyes would drift whenever she recounted this detail. It was always the end to the story. I wish I had asked her *how* she cared for her husband when he was dying, what it was like for her. I am sure that injecting morphine was the least of it.

The practicalities of caring for someone who is dying – dealing with their piss and vomit, blood and shit, their needs for ever-greater doses of symptom-relieving medication – are often too much for family members to attend to – for those who are lucky enough to have families. We do not have anywhere near adequate services to assist families with these tasks. You're lucky if you can get a daily visit from a palliative care or district nurse, or an on-call GP. The maximum assistance you can get in Australia is an hour or two a day.

A physician I know helped her mother die at home. The physician's husband was also a doctor, her daughter a nurse. They had the requisite skills to care for her dying mother. A palliative care nurse visited once a day to titrate the morphine. The physician says of the experience:

> It was enormously distressing, to cope with the physical supports she needed – the washing, the toileting – as well as give the emotional support to her and each other. She was terrified of dying and suffered great psychological and spiritual distress. My husband acted as a surrogate doctor – directing the morphine doses, sometimes based more upon her psychic distress than her pain. This caused him enormous strain and guilt. It would have been better for a doctor outside of the family to guide these decisions, to share some of the weight. For weeks after she died, none of us could go into her room. It stood as a sort of shrine to what was a terribly exhausting and traumatic experience.

We have definitions of a good death. This, from the Grattan Institute report *Dying Well*, is a typical example:

- To know when death is coming, and to understand what can be expected
- To be able to retain control of what happens
- To be afforded dignity and privacy
- To have control over pain relief and other symptom control
- To have choice and control over where death occurs (at home or elsewhere)
- To have access to information and expertise of whatever kind is necessary
- To have access to any spiritual or emotional support required
- To have access to hospice care in any location including home, not only in hospital
- To have control over who is present and who shares the end
- To be able to issue advanced directives that ensure wishes are respected
- To have time to say goodbye, and control over other aspects of timing
- To be able to leave when it is time to go, and not to have life prolonged pointlessly

I read charts such as this and can't help but wonder what a chart outlining a good life would look like, and whether we should attempt to mandate that first. A good death – an ideal death – is pre-planned, perfectly timed, excretion-free, speedy, neat and controlled. Birth is not like this. Life is not like this. And yet we think we have a right to ask it of death.

We want a caesarean-section death. The only way we could come close to meeting all these criteria for a good death would be to put people down when they reach a predetermined age, before the chaos of illness sets in.

People in the last stages of malignancy sometimes have access to services and planning to assist them in their wish to die at home. They follow a different trajectory to death. Some people can afford to pay for their own nursing assistance. In the 1980s people with AIDS often died at home: they died quickly, usually of sepsis, and had large, committed communities to draw upon for support.

For the vast majority of the frail elderly who are hospitalised for treatment of exacerbations and complications of their chronic heart and lung and kidney diseases, it is difficult to know the point at which our treatment will fail. A stint in hospital – and perhaps a hospital death – is what they trade for a chance to get better. And, when it becomes obvious that they are dying, there may be no one to look after them at home. That there is always or most times an alternative to hospital is an illusion.

The statistic often quoted is that because of our ageing population the number of Australians dying each year will double in the coming decades. Part of the impetus to increase the number of people dying at home comes from concern about the future demand for hospital beds, rather than from a benevolent desire to fulfil the wish to die at home. Dying people require care, whether in hospital or not. And it is important to note that even if we do establish adequate services to assist more people to die humanely at home, this will not necessarily prove much cheaper than funding hospital beds. Professor Alison Mudge is a general physician and prolific researcher at the Royal Brisbane Hospital. She said to me recently, "Hospital is not a bad place to die. I used to believe it was, but I no longer think this is the case." To say such a thing is to fly in the face of the orthodoxy that we have medicalised death. She says, "Dying is dying, no matter where you are. People really aren't preoccupied by their environment when they're dying. It's the people around them and the care they receive that matter. And what are we supposed to do? Imagine sending an elderly patient home to die in their housing commission flat, alone."

Not so long ago I looked after a patient named Margaret, who was very similar to my grandmother in her determination to live. "I do not want to die," she said from her bed, her creatinine bolting, her uraemic flap getting worse (a result of her failing kidneys), her troponin 250,000 and her lungs slowly filling with fluid (a result of her failing heart).

"I understand," I said. I crouched down by the bed, so that my face was close to hers. I said, "We will keep trying, but your heart and your kidneys are struggling ... and you might die."

It was hard to say those words: *you might die.* I didn't want it to be true. I didn't want to tell her she was nearing the end of her grand, long life.

Her face filled with fear and her eyes filled with tears, and we paused there, eye to eye, saying nothing. Then she tightened her grip on my hand and whispered, "Thank you for telling me."

After two days of diuresis and antibiotics, Margaret was getting worse. She said she felt very tired and was in a lot of pain. I asked her where her pain was. She said, "Everywhere."

We talked again about the possibility that she might die and the idea of palliative care, and over a day or so we backed off the aggressive medicines and increased the symptom modulators – morphine so she didn't feel asphyxiated and to relieve her pain, a benzodiazepine to decrease her anxiety. The transition was gradual. Margaret was a woman of sound and sharp mind who wanted to squeeze every last drop out of her one and only life on earth.

I went up to check on her after the weekend. I walked onto my general medical ward – one of the most acute wards in a gigantic city hospital – and by the front desk were three nurses and the ward clerk. I asked them how Margaret was doing. Each had something to report: the nurses had arranged a single room. They pointed. It was next to the admin desk, with high visibility for all the staff and a magnificent view across the park. They had tried to get Margaret's daughter a bed but it was against occupational health and safety policy, so they'd found a huge recliner chair and made it up with pillows and blankets. Our ward clerk said, "And I've made sure we're ordering her daughter meals."

I felt so proud of them, eking out a space for this death, appreciating its magnitude. What are we except for the sum of what happens to us and with whom?

People talk about the medicalisation of death as if it is something evil doctors have unleashed on the world. Medicine is charged with robbing death of its cultural and spiritual significance, stripping it of all meaning beyond the blunt organic facts. We house the body until it may be called a corpse and then shunt it to the basement, the morgue. But there is another way to view this. Before World War II, death was generally swift – a result of infection. That is no longer the case. We die slowly. We need assistance. The rise of modern medicine in all its institutionalised forms has followed the culture within which it arose. Death as the job of the clinic is an artefact of our culture: there is no longer a large, support-ive community – spiritual or cultural – to cradle the dying. To help bathe them, care for them, attend to them, and infuse death with a significance and collective meaning. There is often no one, or there is only a handful of loved ones, for whom the job may be too large.

As long as we treat the sick, there will be people who die in hospital. In my experience, most families and patients do not want to go home once dying begins. If they do, services are terribly sparse. Given this, current efforts to reduce hospitalisation are, on the whole, inappropriate and – whether this is stated or not – often driven by concerns that are primarily fiscal.

> What should a society be, so that in his last years a man might still
> be a man? The answer is simple: he would always have to have been
> treated as a man. By the fate it allots to its members who can no
> longer work, society gives itself away – it has always looked upon
> them as so much material. Society confesses that as far as it is con-
> cerned, profit is the only thing that counts, and that its "human-
> ism" is mere window dressing ... Old age exposes the failure of our
> entire civilization ... Once we have understood what the state of the
> aged really is, we cannot satisfy ourselves with calling for a more
> generous "old-age policy," higher pensions, decent housing and
> organized leisure. It is the whole system that is at issue and our
> claim cannot be otherwise than radical – change life itself.
>
> – Simone de Beauvoir, *The Coming of Age*

How do we treat patients without torturing them and yet respect their
wishes, their families' wishes, and the extent of what is medically and
physiologically possible? The answer must always be: it depends. Doctors
are scientists, and as such seek ways to make things in the last months and
years neat and predetermined and cost-effective. We seek to limit treatment that we deem futile. We try to formulate pathways and guidelines
and mathematical predictors of life expectancy and discharge destination.
But no algorithm or flow chart can accommodate the messy intricacies of
dying. No pathway can decide which life is worth living.

We cannot monetise, corporatise and streamline our individual demise,
and we must protect the vulnerable: those who feel they are a burden,
that their living has become a burden – those whom other people feel are
a burden. It is a terrible thing for a society to discard the weak and the
disabled and to justify it by saying they have had their turn. Of course we
should never embark on an action that will cause torture or the prolonga-
tion of suffering a patient cannot bear, but our hospitals are not only for

the young and the fully able-bodied.

Atomisation – fragmentation – is a key tendency of our society, and the key problem. Medicine takes the ill and chops them up as if a person is a walking textbook of distinct chapters: lung, heart, liver, brain, activities-of-daily-living, number of steps in the house, cigarettes smoked, alcohol consumed, blood-sugar level. The community is fragmented into individuals, treatment into levels and places of care: we have separated the social and medical and pretend they are not intricately entwined. Our system is slowly changing: there are efforts to decrease fragmentation of our patients' bodies, of their care, and efforts to improve hospitals to better serve the needs of the patients they treat. To offer truly adequate care, however, will necessitate major system overhauls: better care, not less care. We are and we must continue to change medicine, the ways it practises, splits and treats. But if sustainability and health is what we seek, then the larger project is social and political. We must be willing to invest in long-term plans that will result in collective benefits: better, longer lives.

I try to imagine what someone born in 1920 has seen and felt and lived. I try to imagine some 23-year-old calling *me* cute when I'm ninety. Not that that's likely to happen. More likely, I'll be the difficult patient in bed 17. The unreasonable one, who doesn't want to die and who won't stop demanding – my stick, my glasses, my book they lost in Emergency, a *hot* cup of tea, to go home. The difficult, circumlocutory historian. The one who will have the doctors rolling their eyes and saying: "Yes, dear."

The young rule the world; we stomp around doling out mean rations to the old, the machinery of our secure, quiet bodies purring to us the myth that we will be young forever. And, one by one, my patients retreat to small nursing-home rooms and then slip away. Soon they will all be gone. And then it will be your turn and mine to sit in cells and drink the weak tea they hand out at eleven and two, hoarding biscuits in our fridges. Not dead, yet.

The elderly, the frail *are* our society: they gave birth to us, nourished us, protected us, paid their taxes diligently, went to war, ate bread with sugar when there was no butter. They worked and loved and lived – and can continue to do so. They are our parents and grandparents, our carers and neighbours, and they are every one of us in the not-too-distant future.

Right now, we need the resources to care better for the elderly in the institutions we have imperfectly built, and we need adequate supports and deep social transformation so that many more people can live on in their communities and homes. We must remain aware of our ageism in every program and policy we implement. These changes are of pressing importance and they will ultimately benefit us all. Even if – for now – we believe that we would rather be dead than demented, rather be dead than dependent; rather be dead than grow old.

SOURCES

Thank you to all of my family, colleagues and friends who shared their stories with me and helped immeasurably with my thinking. I offer my particular thanks to Dr Michael Currie, Dr Lisa Mitchell, Dr Michael Oldmeadow, Leonie Oldmeadow, Professor Paul Komesaroff, Michael Cathcart, Dr James Olver, Professor Alison Mudge and the Feik family for your careful (often repeated) reading of drafts, and for your thoughtful comments. I am hugely indebted to you.

The names and identifying details of the patients mentioned herein have been changed to preserve anonymity. The clinical stories are from public hospitals I have worked in across three states of Australia.

1 "We elders have learned a thing or two": Roger Angell, "This Old Man: Life in the nineties," *The New Yorker*, 17 February 2014.

2 "Butler outlines": Robert N. Butler, *Why Survive? Being old in America*, Harper & Row, 1975.

2 "Simone de Beauvoir published": Simone de Beauvoir, *La Vieillesse* (*The Coming of Age*), Gallimard, Paris, 1970.

3 "The swelling ranks of 'greedy geezers'": Linda Marsa, "The longevity gap," *Aeon* (online), 2 July 2014.

3 "One of the most-read articles in the *Atlantic*": Ezekiel Emanuel, "Why I Hope to Die at 75," *The Atlantic*, October 2014.

12 "The outcome was a report": Baroness Julia Neuberger (chair) et al., *More Care Less Pathway: A review of the Liverpool care pathway*, UK government, July 2013; Raymond J. Chan, Joan Webster, Jane Phillips and David C. Currow, "The withdrawal of the Liverpool Care Pathway in the United Kingdom: What are the implications for Australia?", *Medical Journal of Australia*, vol. 200, no. 10, 14 June 2014, p. 573.

13 "a tick-box exercise": Margaret McCartney, "Talking about death is not outrageous—reducing it to a tickbox exercise is," *British Medical Journal*, vol. 349, 29 August 2014.

13 "the declaration of futility, is neither simple nor clear": P.R. Helft, M. Siegler and J. Lantos, "The rise and fall of the futility movement," *New England Journal of Medicine*, vol. 343, 2000, pp. 1575–7.

13 "as in the UK": Nat Lievesley, *Ageism and Age Discrimination in Secondary Health Care in the United Kingdom: A review from the literature*, commissioned by the Department of Health, carried out by the Centre for Policy on Ageing, 2009.

15 "Diligently taking ten different prescribed medications has made them very sick": David G. Le Couteur, "Pharmaco-epistemology for the prescribing geriatrician,"

Australasian Journal on Ageing, vol. 27, no. 1, March 2008, pp. 3–7; Doron Garfinkel and Derelie Mangin, "Feasibility study of a systematic approach for discontinuation of multiple medications in older adults: addressing polypharmacy," *Archives of Internal Medicine*, vol. 170, no. 18, 2010, pp. 1648–54.

17   "a satirical novel": Samuel Shem, *The House of God*, Richard Marek, New York, 1978.

19   "the frail elderly do better in wards dedicated to their care": Michael A.H. Cohen, "Integrated care results in fewer elderly people dying in hospital," *British Medical Journal*, vol. 345, 16 July 2012; Alison Mary M. Mudge, Charles P. Denaro and Peter O'Rourke, "Improving hospital outcomes in patients admitted from residential aged care: Results from a controlled trial," *Age and Ageing*, vol. 41, no. 5, September 2012, pp. 670–3; A. Mudge, S. Laracy, K. Richter & C. Denaro, "Controlled trial of multidisciplinary care teams for acutely ill medical inpatients: Enhanced multidisciplinary care," *International Medical Journal*, vol. 36, no. 9, 2006, pp. 558–63; L.Z. Rubenstein, K.R. Josephson, G.D. Weiland, P.A. English, J.A. Sayre, R.L. Kane, "Effectiveness of a geriatric evaluation unit: A randomised clinical trial," *New England Journal of Medicine*, vol. 311, 1984, pp. 1664–70; I. Scott, "Optimising care of the hospitalised elderly: A literature review and suggestions for future research," *Australia New Zealand Journal of Medicine*, vol. 29, no. 2, 1999, pp. 254–63; A.E. Stuck, A.L. Siu, G.D. Wieland, J. Adams, L.Z. Rubinstein, "Comprehensive geriatric assessment: A meta-analysis of controlled trials," *The Lancet*, vol. 342, no. 8878, 1993, pp. 1032–6.

19   "The single most important aspect of care": C.P. Denaro and A. Mudge, "Should geriatric medicine remain a specialty? No," *British Medical Journal*, vol. 337, 12 July 2008.

19   "One reason aged patients do poorly": Jan Savage and Cherill Scott, "Patients' nutritional care in hospital: An ethnographic study of nurses' role and patients' experience," RCN Institute, final report, May 2005.

20   "inappropriately prescribed far too many drugs": Denis O'Mahony, David O'Sullivan, Stephen Byrne, Marie Noelle O'Connor, Cristin Ryan and Paul Gallagher, "STOPP/START criteria for potentially inappropriate prescribing in older people: Version 2," *Age and Ageing* (online), 4 July 2014.

20   "Twenty to thirty per cent of all hospital admissions": Libby Roughead, Susan Semple and Ellie Rosenfeld, *Australian Commission on Safety and Quality in Health Care Literature Review: Medication Safety in Australia*, August 2013.

20   "three things the hospital environment specifically hinders": Alison M. Mudge, Prudence McRae and Mark Cruickshank, "Eat Walk Engage: An Interdisciplinary Collaborative Model to Improve Care of Hospitalized Elders," *American Journal of*

Medical Quality (online), 22 November 2013; NHS, *Five Year Forward View*, 23 October 2014.

21   "hospitals precipitate adverse outcomes": Morton C. Creditor, "Hazards of hospitalization of the elderly," *Annals of Internal Medicine*, vol. 118, no. 3, 1993, pp. 219–23.

22   "concept of futility": P.R. Helft, M. Siegler and J. Lantos, "The rise and fall of the futility movement," *New England Journal of Medicine*, vol. 343, 2000, pp. 1575–7.

22   "reams of data show": Terri R. Fried, John O'Leary, Peter Van Ness and Liana Fraenkel, "Inconsistency over time in the preferences of older persons with advanced illness for life-sustaining treatment," *Journal of the American Geriatrics Society*, vol. 55, no. 7, July 2007, pp. 1007–14.

22   "reams of data": E.P. Cherniack, "Increasing use of DNR orders in the elderly worldwide: Whose choice is it?", *Journal of Medical Ethics*, vol. 28, no. 5, October 2002, pp. 303–7.

23   "good data on treatments such as cardiopulmonary resuscitation": S. Cooper, M. Janghorbani and G. Cooper, "A decade of in-hospital resuscitation: Outcomes and prediction of survival?", *Resuscitation*, vol. 68, no. 2, February 2006, pp. 231–7; P.S. Chan et al. "Long-term outcomes in elderly survivors of in-hospital cardiac arrest," *The New England Journal of Medicine*, vol. 368, 14 March 2013, pp. 1019–26.

27   "Take, for example": Louise Aronson, "The human lifecycle's neglected stepchild," *The Lancet*, vol. 385, no. 9967, 7 February 2015, pp. 500–501.

28   "The truth is dying": Peter Saul, "A conversation that promises savings worth dying for," *The Conversation* (online), 29 April 2013.

29   "their regular use of hospitals and doctors generally, declines": Alastair Gray, "Population Ageing and Health Care Expenditure," *Ageing Horizons*, no. 2, 2005, pp. 15–20.

29   "We spend mostly the same amount": Australian Government Productivity Commission, *An Ageing Australia: Preparing for the Future*, research paper, 22 November 2013; M. Seshamani and A.M. Gray, "A longitudinal study of the effects of age and time to death on hospital costs," *Journal of Health Economics*, vol. 23, no. 2, 2004, pp. 217–35.

29   "not in fact very much": Michael D. Coory, "Ageing and healthcare costs in Australia: A case of policy-based evidence?", *Medical Journal of Australia*, vol. 180, no. 11, 7 June 2004, pp. 581–3.

29   "Data from New South Wales": Katina Kardamanidis, Kim Lim, Cristalyn Da Cunha, Lee K. Taylor and Louisa R. Jorm, "Hospital costs of older people in New South Wales in the last year of life," *Medical Journal of Australia*, vol. 187, no. 7, 2007, pp. 383–6.

29 "costs associated with the last year of life actually fall": N. G. Levinsky, W. Yu, A. Ash, M. Moskowitz, G. Gazelle, O. Saynina, O. & E.J. Emanuel, "Influence of age on Medicare expenditures and medical care in the last year of life," *Journal of the American Medical Association*, vol. 286, no. 11, 2001, pp. 1349–55.

29 "currently rising at a far slower rate": Australian Institute of Health and Welfare, *Health expenditure Australia 2012–13*, media release, 23 September 2014.

30 "according to another AIHW report": *AIHW, Healthy Life Expectancy in Australia: Patterns and trends 1998 to 2012*, media release, 21 November 2014.

30 "seek to minimise current financing": Michael D. Coory, "Ageing and healthcare costs in Australia: a case of policy-based evidence?", *Medical Journal of Australia*, vol. 180, no. 11, 2004, pp. 581–3.

30 "real areas of waste": S.R. Hill, D.D. Henry and A.J. Smith, "Rising prescription drug costs: whose responsibility?", *Medical Journal of Australia*, vol. 167, no. 1, 1997, pp. 6–7.

30 "widespread international agreement that we should now be spending more … on integration of care and on prevention": N. Goodwin et al., "A report to the department of health and the NHS future forum. Integrated care for patients and populations: improving outcomes by working together," The King's Fund and Nuffield Trust, London, 2012; Gareth Iacobucci, "NHS plan calls for new models of care and greater emphasis on prevention," *British Medical Journal*, vol. 349, 2014; Jeremiah A. Barondess, "On the preservation of health," *Journal of the American Medical Association*, vol. 294, no. 23, 2005, pp. 3024–6; David Oliver, Catherine Foot and Richard Humphries, "Making our health and care systems fit for an ageing population," *Age and Ageing*, vol. 43, no. 5, March 2014.

30 "rate their own health as good": Australian Bureau of Statistics, *Australian Health Survey: Updated Results, 2011–12 — Australia*, Cat. No. 43640DO001_20112012, ABS, 30 July 2013.

30 "spending more years of their longer lives in good health": Andrew Steptoe, Angus Deaton and Arthur A. Stone, "Subjective wellbeing, health, and ageing," *The Lancet*, vol. 385, no. 9968, 14 February 2015, pp. 640–8.

30 "should be urgently addressing the poor health of the younger generations": Kaarin Jane Anstey et al., "The influence of smoking, sedentary lifestyle and obesity on cognitive impairment-free life expectancy," *International Journal of Epidemiology* (online), 22 August 2014, pp. 1–10; *Living Longer. Living Better: Macroeconomic implications of population ageing and selected policy responses*, Commonwealth of Australia, 2012; John R. Beard and David E Bloom, "Towards a comprehensive public health response to population ageing," *The Lancet*, vol. 385, no. 9968, 14 February 2015, pp. 658–61; David E. Bloom et al., "Macroeconomic implications of

population ageing and selected policy responses," *The Lancet*, vol. 385, no. 9968, 14 February 2015, pp. 649–57; Somnath Chatterji et al., "Health, functioning, and disability in older adults – present status and future implications," vol. 385, no. 9967, 7 February 2015, pp. 563–75; K. Ritchie et al., "Designing prevention programmes to reduce incidence of dementia: Prospective cohort study of modifiable risk factors," *British Medical Journal*, vol. 341, 2010, p. 3885.

30   "six modifiable risk factors": V. Kontis et al., "Contribution of six risk factors to achieving the 25×25 non-communicable disease mortality reduction targets: A modelling study," *The Lancet*, vol. 384, no. 9941, 2 August 2014, pp. 427–37.

32   Atul Gawande, *Being Mortal: Medicine and what matters in the end*, Metropolitan Books, Henry Holt & Co., New York, 2014.

32   "Almost all medical professionals have seen": Ken Murray, "How doctors choose to die," *The Guardian*, 9 February 2012.

32   "A frail, elderly man": Jeanne Erdmann, "Why is death denied to the terminally ill?", *Aeon* (online), 15 December 2014.

33   "a recent King's Fund review": N. Goodwin et al., *A Report to the Department of Health and the NHS Future Forum: Integrated care for patients and populations: improving outcomes by working together*, The King's Fund and Nuffield Trust, London, 2012.

33   "it is widely known and reported": A. Bowling, "Ageism in cardiology," *British Medical Journal*, vol. 319, 1999, pp. 1353–5; M.B. Hamel et al. "Patient age and decisions to withhold life-sustaining treatments from seriously ill, hospitalized adults: SUPPORT Investigators: Study to understand prognoses and preferences for outcomes and risks of treatment," *Annals of Internal Medicine*, vol. 130, no. 2, January 1999, pp. 116–25; Michael Rivlin, "Should age based rationing of health care be illegal?", *British Medical Journal*, vol. 319, no. 7221, 1999, p. 1379.

33   "A recent article in the *Lancet*": Louise Aronson, "The human lifecycle's neglected stepchild," *The Lancet*, vol. 385, no. 9967, 7 February 2015, pp. 500–501.

34   "a recent large study in the United States": Peter K. Lindenauer et al. "Outcomes associated with invasive and noninvasive ventilation among patients hospitalized with exacerbations of chronic obstructive pulmonary disease," *JAMA Internal Medicine*, vol. 174, no. 12, 2014, pp. 1982–93.

35   "Preventable over-treatment": Erik Nord, Jeff Richardson and Helga Kuhse, *Maximising Health Benefits Versus Egalitarianism: An Australian survey of health issues*, Centre for Health Program Evaluation, working paper 45.

36   "rationing is a hugely controversial issue": National Health and Medical Research Council, *Ethical Considerations Relating to Health Care Resource Allocation Decisions*, Commonwealth of Australia, 1993.

37   "The Supreme Court": Lindy Willmott, Ben White, Malcolm K. Smith and Dom-

inic J. C. Wilkinson, "Withholding and withdrawing life-sustaining treatment in a patient's best interests: Australian judicial deliberations," *Medical Journal of Australia*, vol. 201, no. 9, 3 November 2014, pp. 545–7.

39–40 "Hundreds of millions, probably billions": Amanda Vanstone, "Facing what's at the very heart of life and death," *The Age*, 27 April 2014.

45 "No one wants to be a 'burden'": Joan Didion, "The Case of Theresa Schiavo," *The New York Review of Books*, 9 June 2005.

47 "My mother had been": Paul Komesaroff, *Experiments in Love and Death*, MUP, Melbourne, 2008.

47 "Studies show": Angela Fagerlin and Carl E. Schneider, *The Failure of the Living Will*, Hastings Centre report, March–April 2004.

48 "Who's to know if they changed their mind": Terri R. Fried, John O'Leary, Peter Van Ness, and Liana Fraenkel, "Inconsistency over time in the preferences of older persons with advanced illness for life-sustaining treatment," *Journal of the American Geriatrics Society*, vol. 55, no. 7, July 2007, pp. 1007–14.

48–9 "Suppose, for example, that you sign a directive": Thomas Nagel, "In whose interest?", in L.W. Sumner, *Assisted Death: A study in ethics and law*, Oxford, 2011.

49 "The promotion of advance care planning": Nicholas Talley, "Where are the health policies?", opinion piece, Royal Australian College of Physicians, 12 September 2013.

51 "Both my mother and her sister": John Hardwig, "Medicalization and Death," *APA Newsletter*, vol. 6, no. 1, Fall 2006.

51 "Last week, I performed": Gabriel Weston, "Developing judgment, not being judgmental," *The Lancet*, vol. 385, no. 9963, 10 January 2015, pp. 108–9.

54 "About a quarter of Australians over the age of eighty-five": Australian Institute of Health and Welfare, *Residential Aged Care in Australia 2010–11: A statistical overview released*, media release, AIHW, 19 September 2012.

54 "Dementia is the reason half of them have been institutionalised": Australian Human Rights Commission, *Respect and Choice: A Human rights approach for ageing and health*, AHRC, 2012.

54 "Ageism is rife": Susan Ryan, "The Rights of Older People and Age Discrimination in Australia," speech given at the Australian Association of Gerontology National Conference, Brisbane Convention and Exhibition Centre, 22 November 2012.

55 "She spent her last days": Josh Planos, "The Dutch village where everyone has dementia," *The Atlantic*, 14 November 2014.

55 "Mild symptoms can be prevented": Margaret Lock, *The Alzheimer Conundrum: Entanglements of Dementia and Aging*, Princeton University Press, 2013.

55 "far more expensive and complex": Anne Corbett, Alistair Burns and Clive Ballard, "Don't use antipsychotics routinely to treat agitation and aggression in people with dementia," *British Medical Journal*, vol. 349, 3 November 2014.

55 B.R. Levy, M.D. Slade, S.R. Kunkel and S.V. Kasl, "Longevity increased by positive self-perceptions of aging," *Journal of Personality and Social Psychology*, vol. 83, no. 2, 2002, pp. 261–70.

56 "I'd go home thinking": *It Takes A Community: A relationship-focused approach to celebrating and supporting old age*, Fire Films, 2014, www.youtube.com/watch?v=IUJWFWXz-wY&feature=youtu.be

56 "De Hogeweyk": Josh Planos, "The Dutch village where everyone has dementia," *The Atlantic*, 14 November 2014.

58 "largest proportion of elderly citizens": "An Ageing Australia: Preparing for the Future," Productivity Commission Research Paper, 22 November 2013.

58 "Fureai kippu": Mayumi Hayashi, "Japan's Fureai Kippu: Time-Banking in Elderly Care: Origins, development, challenges and impact," *International Journal of Community Currency Research*, vol. 16, Section A 30-X, 2012.

58 "2.8 per cent of Japan's aged currently reside in nursing homes": OECD, "Health at a Glance 2013," *OECD Indicators*, 21 November 2013.

62 "Only 14 per cent of people in Australia die at home": Hal Swerisson and Stephen Duckett, *Dying Well*, Grattan Institute, Report No. 2014–10, September 2014.

64 "To know when death is coming": Swerisson and Duckett, 2014, p. 8.

65 "not necessarily prove much cheaper": E. Emanuel, et al., "The Economics of Dying: The Illusion of cost saving at the end of life," *New England Journal of Medicine*, vol. 330, 24 February 1994, pp. 540–544.

67 "death was generally swift – a result of infection": J. Lynn, "Learning to Care for People with Chronic Illness Facing the End of Life," *The Journal of the American Medical Association*, vol. 284, no. 19, 2000, pp. 2508–11.

68 "What should a society be": Simone de Beauvoir, *La Vieillesse* (The Coming of Age), Gallimard, Paris, 1970.

Other references

"Ageism in services for transient ischaemic attack and stroke," *British Medical Journal*, editorial, vol. 333, 7 September 2006, pp. 508–9.

Australian Institute of Health and Welfare, *Health expenditure Australia 2012–13*, media release, AIHW, 23 September 2014.

Australian Institute of Health and Welfare, *Australia's health 2014*, AIHW, 25 June 2014.

Australian Institute of Health and Welfare, *Dementia Care in Hospitals: Costs and Strategies*, media release, AIHW, 14 March 2013.

David Brindle, "Older people are an asset, not a drain," *The Guardian*, 2 March 2011.

Andrew Clegg et al., "Frailty in elderly people," *The Lancet*, vol. 381, no. 9868, 2 March 2013, pp. 752–62.

John Daley, *Game-changers: Economic reform priorities for Australia*, Grattan Institute, 8 June 2012.

Lisa Guenther, "The concrete abyss," *Aeon* (online), 16 April 2014.

Margaret McCartney, *Living with Dying: finding care and compassion at the end of life*, Pinter and Martin, 2014.

Wendy Moyle and Siobhan O'Dwyer, "Quality of life in people living with dementia in nursing homes," *Current Opinions in Psychiatry*, vol. 25, 2012, pp. 480–4.

Alison M. Mudge, Peter O'Rourke and Charles P. Denaro, "Timing and risk factors for functional changes associated with medical hospitalization in older patients," *The Journal of Gerontology, Biological Sciences and Medical Sciences*, vol. 65A, no. 8, 2010, pp. 866–72.

The old women's project (online resource), www.oldwomensproject.org

Phoebe Weaver Williams, *Age Discrimination in the Delivery of Health Care Services to Our Elders*, Marquette University Law School, faculty publications, 2009.

Richard Denniss

Two-thirds of Australian adults didn't vote for Tony Abbott. Democracy doesn't work the way we are told it does, and the conservatives who oppose virtually all constitutional change rage against senators for doing exactly what the framers of the constitution envisaged they would do.

In his illuminating analysis of the history and politics of Clive Palmer, Guy Rundle made none of the above points. But by placing his analysis of the leader of the Palmer United Party (PUP) within a broader analysis of the Australian body politic, Rundle's essay forces us to look carefully not just at Clive Palmer, but at the performance of our parliamentary democracy in its totality.

Rundle sets himself apart from the pack with his premise that Clive Palmer is an inevitable consequence of the strains our democratic system is under, rather than the cause of those strains. That is, rather than lay the blame for the "chaos" of the current parliament at the feet of the billionaire who "bought his way into parliament," Rundle instead points the finger at the caste of political insiders whom he sees as so removed from the concerns of ordinary Australians that they are unable to comprehend, let alone respond to, the electoral appeal of Clive Palmer, Nick Xenophon, the Greens or the growing number of independents who find themselves in state and federal parliaments. Rundle brings an outsider's eye to the insider game of political commentary, and he observes that our democratic emperors are not only stark naked, but in poor health as well.

The clearest evidence that Australia's democracy is ailing is the fact that in a country with so-called "compulsory" voting, at the 2013 election only 75 per cent of adult Australians cast a valid vote. There are 2.3 million voting-age Australians who are not enrolled to vote (some being residents who never registered for full citizenship, others full citizens who just never registered), a further 1 million who are registered but didn't bother to show up, and a further 800,000 who voted informally. All up, the 4.1 million adults who cast no valid vote is neck and neck with the 4.3 million who voted for the ALP and is fast closing in on the votes cast for the Coalition.

When you combine those who didn't vote for Tony Abbott's Coalition government with those who didn't vote at all, it becomes obvious why it is so hard to find someone who is enthusiastic about the Abbott government's "mandate." Fully two-thirds of adult Australians did not vote for his government at the 2013 election. If the disenfranchised voters of Australia could be bothered forming a political party, it would be a major party.

The accusation that modern politicians are "poll-driven" is now so common that it barely receives examination. Why then, given that 90 per cent of Australians support a ban on junk-food advertising during children's viewing hours, does neither of our major parties support such a ban? Shouldn't poll-driven politicians jump on the opportunity to do something that would cost the budget nothing, save the health budget a fortune and make so many voters happy? No chance.

Similarly, given that 99 per cent of Australians earn less than $300,000 per annum, why wouldn't the major parties support reform of the tax system to raise revenue from the 1 per cent in order to fund services for the 99 per cent? Why wouldn't the major parties chase votes promising to come down hard on rorting of superannuation and capital-gains tax concessions? Again, no chance.

In examining both the trajectory of Clive Palmer's political life, and the environment in which he wields political power, Rundle's essay sheds harsh light on the extent to which the established political parties have silently decided to agree on a wide range of issues. The voting public (and the non-voting public) are significantly more concerned with population growth, free trade agreements, corporate donations and the rise of corporate power in Australia than the leaders of the ALP and the Coalition.

But when neither the prime minister nor the Opposition leader will take an issue seriously, then it is a rare individual or non-government organisation that can manage to get the media to do so. Clive Palmer is one such individual.

While bipartisan political determination to ignore an issue might be enough to silence the media, it is not, however, sufficient to assuage community concern. Indeed, the harder the insiders work to stifle debate on big issues, the more they marginalise the political appeal of the once major parties. Put simply, the major parties' control over what they talk about is not the same as control over what the public care about.

There is a straightforward economic explanation for the convergence of the ALP and the Coalition on many issues. In 1929 Harold Hotelling spelt out the "principle of minimum differentiation" in order to explain, among other things, why ice-cream vendors on a beach might cluster in the middle of the beach rather than spread out along it.

The principle goes like this: imagine a one-kilometre beach with two ice-cream vendors, each 333 metres from opposite ends. Assuming that sunbathers are evenly spread out along the beach, the vendors' decision to position themselves in such a way ensures that both vendors will get 50 per cent market share, while minimising the distance that any beachgoer has to carry a melting ice-cream back to their kids.

Now imagine that the southern ice-cream van moves 50 metres closer to the centre of the beach. They will still be the closest to the sunbakers at the southern tip of the beach, but they will also pick up some new customers from the middle. Of course, the rational response of the northern ice-cream van is for it to start heading south, until – you guessed it – both vans wind up parked next to each other in the middle.

While it makes perfect sense for duopolists to cluster near each other, this means that the big players are always vulnerable to "new entrants" taking market share on their flanks. The coalition of the Liberals and the Nationals is specifically designed to manage such splintering on the right, while the ALP and the Greens are unwilling, or unable, to broker a similar deal to divvy up the "left" market and allocate the spoils. (Note: the Nationals, who poll 4 per cent of the primary vote, nominate the deputy prime minister when the Coalition is in government.)

As the major parties chase the same votes in the middle, it is inevitable that they will move further away from their bases. With compulsory preferential voting, however, political parties can do what ice-cream vendors only dream of: they can force people to take the long walk across hot sand to vote for them.

Rundle talks about the mutual benefit that incumbent political parties receive from designing electoral rules that help protect the political market from new entrants. Indeed, he describes the "triple lock" that helps entrench their political power and market share: compulsory voting, preferential voting and taxpayer funding of incumbent political parties.

Ice-cream vendors who get too far away from their customers run the risk that their customers will choose to go without rather than go on a long hike. Rundle rightly credits (blames) compulsory voting for forcing us to buy metaphorical ice-cream. But, as discussed above, a large and growing number of voters are opting out.

As Rundle makes clear, the media have, on the whole, missed both the decline in democratic participation and the steady rise in electoral support for minor parties and independents. Unlike much of the Canberra press gallery, Rundle analyses the emergence of Clive Palmer in the context of such trends and, in turn, draws more interesting conclusions about both the strategy and prospects of the PUP than those whose analysis of the crossbench starts from the premise that the PUP are illegitimate self-promoters who have simply "gamed the system."

There are some good reasons for gallery journalists to focus on the priorities of the prime minister and the Opposition leader and to pay less attention to the motivations and strategies of the crossbench. The constitutional power of prime ministers, for example, is in no way limited by the proportion of the electorate that voted for them. Similarly, when there is no chance of parliament debating junk-food advertising or population growth, it is understandable that political reporters don't bother discussing such issues.

The problem arises, however, when political commentators conflate the set of issues the major parties are willing to discuss with the set of issues of interest to newspaper readers and the population more generally. Experienced gallery journalists simply "know" that population growth, for example, is a "non-issue." Significantly, however, this knowledge comes not from a careful examination of the concerns of voters, but from a long history of watching senior politicians ignore the issue.

Pauline Hanson provided an explosive example of what can happen when an independent decides to give political voice to an issue the major parties had decided not to discuss. The rise of far-right parties in Europe since the global financial crisis provides a range of examples of what happens when the public thinks that the major parties of Europe are determined to limit the problems that are up for discussion or limit the range of solutions that warrant consideration. Again, stifling debate in the parliament should not be confused, by politicians or journalists, with winning a debate in the community.

The Australian Senate was explicitly designed by the authors of our constitution to act as a check on the power of the government of the day. It was specifically designed to ensure that the smaller states were overrepresented, and it was specifically given the power to block not just legislation, but the passage of money bills. Malcolm Fraser's Liberal Party famously used all of those powers not merely to obstruct, but to destroy the Whitlam government. Presumably, such use of Senate powers was "OK" because it was a major party that used them, and a "conservative" major party at that.

For decades, independents and minor parties have used the Senate not just to block legislation, but to scrutinise government performance, to amend legislation

Never again miss an issue. Subscribe and save.

☐ **1 year subscription** (4 issues) $59 (incl. GST). Subscriptions outside Australia $89.
All prices include postage and handling.

☐ **2 year subscription** (8 issues) $105 (incl. GST). Subscriptions outside Australia $165.
All prices include postage and handling.

☐ Tick here to commence subscription with the current issue.

PAYMENT DETAILS I enclose a cheque/money order made out to Schwartz Publishing Pty Ltd.
Or please debit my credit card (MasterCard, Visa or Amex accepted).

CARD NO.

EXPIRY DATE   /   CCV   AMOUNT $

CARDHOLDER'S NAME

SIGNATURE

NAME

ADDRESS

EMAIL   PHONE

tel: (03) 9486 0288 **fax:** (03) 9486 0244 **email:** subscribe@blackincbooks.com **www.quarterlyessay.com**

An inspired gift. Subscribe a friend.

☐ **1 year subscription** (4 issues) $59 (incl. GST). Subscriptions outside Australia $89.
All prices include postage and handling.

☐ **2 year subscription** (8 issues) $105 (incl. GST). Subscriptions outside Australia $165.
All prices include postage and handling.

☐ Tick here to commence subscription with the current issue.

PAYMENT DETAILS I enclose a cheque/money order made out to Schwartz Publishing Pty Ltd.
Or please debit my credit card (MasterCard, Visa or Amex accepted).

CARD NO.

EXPIRY DATE   /   CCV   AMOUNT $

CARDHOLDER'S NAME   SIGNATURE

NAME

ADDRESS

EMAIL   PHONE

RECIPIENT'S NAME

RECIPIENT'S ADDRESS

tel: (03) 9486 0288 **fax:** (03) 9486 0244 **email:** subscribe@blackincbooks.com **www.quarterlyessay.com**

Delivery Address:
37 LANGRIDGE St
COLLINGWOOD VIC 3066

Quarterly Essay
Reply Paid 79448
COLLINGWOOD VIC 3066

No stamp required
if posted in Australia

Delivery Address:
37 LANGRIDGE St
COLLINGWOOD VIC 3066

Quarterly Essay
Reply Paid 79448
COLLINGWOOD VIC 3066

and to give voice to issues that governments would prefer not to discuss. Unlike Fraser's Liberals, if crossbench senators use their constitutional power to vote down legislation, they are typically accused of "wrecking" things and causing "chaos," rather than simply doing their job. Do conservative commentators and business groups really want taxpayers to spend hundreds of millions of dollars electing and supporting senators who rubber-stamp whatever governments, including ALP governments, want to do?

There is now widespread support for reform of the way senators are elected, but why stop there? Why not inquire into why so many people no longer vote? Why not inquire into what, if anything, the Australian Electoral Commission is doing to find millions of non-voters and remind them of their obligations? Why not survey the non-voters to ask them what would be required to draw them back into our body politic? Why not have a Senate inquiry into the state of our democracy? The political caste would hate it.

In *The Usual Suspects*, Kevin Spacey's character said the greatest trick the devil ever pulled was to convince the world he didn't exist. The greatest trick that Rundle's political caste has played is to convince the public that politics is boring and policy is something made by experts.

While some politicians can be boring, politics isn't. In a democracy, politics is how fights between powerful (and not so powerful) players are settled. Anyone who tells you politics is boring either isn't watching closely, or doesn't want you to watch at all.

Richard Denniss

Note: I was described in Rundle's essay as a former chief-of-staff to Greens leader Christine Milne; I was not. I was chief-of-staff to Senator Natasha Stott Despoja when she was leader of the Australian Democrats, and strategy adviser to the then leader of the Greens, Senator Bob Brown.

Tad Tietze

Late in *Clivosaurus*, Guy Rundle warns against over-interpreting his subject and argues that it "would be an error ... to seek to find in Palmer's life the key to his current hold on the political process" and that he "is not a cause of our current fractured politics: he is one of its most spectacular effects."

Unfortunately, for most of the rest of the essay, Guy ignores his own advice and ends up missing the most salient factors driving the Palmer phenomenon, as well as failing to grasp its weaknesses.

Perhaps most tellingly, for an intervention that purports to explain Palmer's success, Guy's essay has almost nothing in it about who actually voted for Palmer, or why. Instead, Guy tries to anatomise Palmer's idiosyncratic politics through a mixture of retelling his life story in the context of a rough sketch of Australian, Queensland and Gold Coast social and political history, observing Clive speak to public audiences (Guy never gets a personal interview), quoting various journalists' disapproving op-eds, and recounting the big man's often erratic pronouncements and manoeuvres. All this is leavened with more than a little wishful projection about Palmer's progressive side, because – as Guy cannot avoid acknowledging – the contradictions of the PUP leader's program are hard to miss.

Guy's descriptions of Palmer's personal quirks and obsessions leave us with a portrait that could have been drawn of any number of second-string political operators from the Queensland National Party's Joh-era heyday. There is certainly nothing specific about Clive's politics that could explain how he's had so much electoral impact. So it's no wonder that Guy ends up taking a soft swipe at Palmer's ability to use his wealth to "buy" an election, a complaint more commonly heard from politicos shameless enough to attack others for injecting self-interest and big money into politics.

You cannot satisfactorily explain the PUP's success without grasping a deeper process of the breakdown of the political arrangements that dominated Australia during most of the twentieth century. Until things started to unravel in the late years of the post–World War II boom, democratic politics had a mass social base, organised around the pivot of Labourism, which rested on powerful but deeply conservative trade union organisations in civil society. Both left and right defined themselves in relation to this social fact, which provided stability even when major shocks like war and depression intervened.

Perhaps the key accelerator of the decomposition of this political order, and the hollowing out of the social base of the political class as a whole, was the thirteen years of union "Accord" under the Hawke and Keating governments. Labor's working-class base suffered real wage decline in the service of a massive upward redistribution of wealth. Yet this was also the high point of Labourism, with mass sacrifice traded for unparalleled governmental influence for union leaders. It exhausted any distinct Labor Party and trade union relevance to workers – unionisation now plumbs depths not seen since the beginning of last century – as well as leaving the conservatives with no distinct agenda of their own, Labor having delivered so well for business without their involvement.

If there was ever a period of "neoliberal" hegemony in Australia, it was over by the time Keating turned on a dime and campaigned successfully as the anti-economic rationalist against a hapless John Hewson, who was, after all, just trying to continue what Labor had started. Since then, the major parties have had to deal with their declining authority in the electorate by largely avoiding big-bang economic reforms, a fact which troubles commentators desperate for a replay of the glorious 1980s. Yet this political caution has not halted the contraction of stable voter bases, rising electoral volatility, falling party memberships, increasing segregation of a political class with little "real world" experience, growing reliance on public funding of politics and, perhaps most worryingly, mounting voter detachment from politics.

Such developments have driven the dissolution of right–left allegiances, followed over time by the rise of new political forces tapping into public discontent with politicians, who are increasingly seen as self-obsessed and lacking relevance to people's lives. These new formations, from less stable entities like One Nation to more enduring ones like the Greens, have gained by cannibalising the fragmenting bases of one or other major party, or appealing to the anti-political mood of the electorate, or usually a bit of both.

It is impossible to understand how Palmer could come from nowhere to get 5.5 per cent of the national vote in 2013 unless you recognise that his success rested much less on any positive agenda than on something almost entirely negative: the long-run erosion of the old political order.

Guy is unable to acknowledge this political crack-up in any substantive sense. So he tends to attribute the rise of parties like the Greens to the growth of a new "class of knowledge/culture/policy producers" (even though the vast bulk of this demographic group still votes for the major parties), rather than the breakdown of Labor's political hold in certain geographic locales. He also downplays the generalised anti-political mood in society, which is now so obvious that even the commentariat and the polite middle classes talk about it openly.

At one level this rejection of "anti-politics" as an explanation is not surprising. Guy makes pretty clear he is looking for a way to revive politics as a reflection of "the general will" of society, rather than considering the possibility it's actually not really about that kind of thing at all. Furthermore, he seems to associate anti-politics with "angry resistance" to the mainstream, when in fact what marks developments in recent years is the *detached* quality of the punishment meted out by voters.

Guy quotes a much-discussed 2014 Lowy Institute poll showing high levels of dissatisfaction with democracy. I'll add what researchers found when they asked *why* people felt this way: the two top responses were "democracy is not working because there is no real difference between the policies of the major parties" and "democracy only serves the interests of a few and not the majority of society." Despite this, Guy proposes tweaks to electoral processes to make them more technically representative, rather than something more fundamental. He also speculates:

> What if Tony Abbott receives a distinct majority of the vote in 2016, but Labor wins one more seat, and the government is decided, in Labor's favour, by an informal caucus of Adam Bandt, Andrew Wilkie and Clive Palmer, who can also guarantee the new government a working majority in the Senate? Would the Coalition accept that very, very possible scenario as legitimate? More to the point, would their supporters outside the political caste?
>
> Maybe it will take an event of that magnitude to shake us from our complacency, our mistaking of torpor and disengagement for orderliness and legitimacy. If so, bring it on.

This is no more than a replay of 2010–13, with hardly any of the names changed, but Guy has nothing explicit to say about why the last government was such a depressing political failure. After all, it opened the way for an Opposition leader as disliked as Abbott to become prime minister, and led to a large drop in the left's vote and the rise of Palmer, the latter delivering a large chunk of former Labor votes to Abbott via preferences. Palmer's program didn't matter anywhere near as much as his ability to play to the popular disdain for both the government (with the Greens frittering away anti-establishment credibility by propping it up) and the Opposition. The PUP generally did best in the working-class suburbs of big cities: that sea of swinging voters endlessly mythologised by the old parties. According to analysis by Peter Brent, the PUP's ability to harvest votes from Labor was on display again in the West Australian Senate by-election, this time in the context of a falling Coalition vote and Greens revival.

Following these wins, rather than copy Labor's partisan hectoring about the "lies" and "broken promises" of the May budget – as if no previous government had committed such sins and convinced voters of the necessity of reforms any-way – Palmer told *Lateline*'s Tony Jones, "This is an ideological budget, it's just about ideology and about smashing someone. It's not really about what's best for the country." It was a supremely anti-political moment, fingering Abbott for hurting the country by playing to his side's fixations. It came as the PUP's popularity scaled closer to its July 2014 peak in the context of high-visibility manoeuvres on the floor of parliament.

Despite Palmer's appeals to widely held values associated with the political centre, his ability to take on the government rested not on popular support, but on the conservatives' lack of authority. This authority problem was something that wrong-footed LNP supporters, because the right had won a nominally large two-party-preferred victory over a shambolic (but, thanks to Rudd's return, still viable) Labor Party. The PUP leader's own lack of a base gave him space to play the anti-politics card as a form of pure politics, free of dreary constraints like the views of a membership or dissenting voices in the party room, let alone a stable constituency.

But after July, as it became more apparent that the Coalition would deal with Palmer rather than simply try to monster him, his eagerness to play backroom negotiator began to undermine his image as an anti-political crusader. As the PUP's poll numbers fell, the constant hostile media barrage suddenly seemed to have an impact. Finally, fearing their own premature political mortality if they tagged along with their leader's increasingly cuddly approach to the govern-ment, Jacqui Lambie and Ricky Muir pulled away, with the Tasmanian senator opting for an open split.

Because Guy is entranced by the virtues of the Clive Palmer he has con-structed in his mind, he misses why, even by the time he filed his essay on 1 November, the writing was on the wall for the PUP, with its poor polling and mounting internal problems. As Kevin Rudd's ignominious demise in 2010 demonstrated, those who fail to deliver on implicit promises to shake up a reviled political system quickly fall foul of the voters. It is too soon to tell whether voters have passed a final judgment on Palmer as their representative *contra* the political class. But either way, the mood that he was able to tap into shows no sign of dissipating.

Across much of the Western world, this mood has become the new normal. It has meant rising anxiety for political classes as they seek ways to manage their populations without even the appearance of looking after people's social interests. Perhaps the most spectacular example of this has been in Spain, where millions were involved in the explicitly anti-political 15-M social movement, and where the recently formed Podemos party – which campaigns on the basis of expelling the entire "political caste" – leads some national polls. Things are nowhere near as acute in Australia, but chronic political turmoil has provoked growing concern among elites that the country may become ungovernable should a serious reform program need to be undertaken. This breakdown, more profound than Guy's shallow reading of a temporarily unresponsive political process, is what made possible Palmer's rise.

Tad Tietze

Paul Cleary

The single most extraordinary fact about Clive Palmer and his conflated business and political interests is that he took $10 million from his Chinese government–owned joint venture partner to fund his political party, which now holds considerable influence in the Senate.

Nothing like this has ever happened before in Australian political history, but the sheer gobsmacking significance of it will be lost on readers of Guy Rundle's *Clivosaurus*, where it is mentioned only in passing. Palmer's use of Citic Pacific's money for electoral purposes is noted just three times in the essay, and each reference is one sentence long. Rundle doesn't even state the amount of money involved.

This pivotal issue is the centre of a Supreme Court action brought by Citic, an investigation by the West Australian police, and has seen Palmer storm out of several TV interviews, yet not only does Rundle blithely bypass it, he also shirks rigorous analysis of Palmer's business interests and finances.

Rundle is a former editor of left-wing magazine *Arena* and is now described as a roving correspondent for Crikey. A big part of the problem with this essay is that he isn't the right person to have written it. When it comes to Palmer, he lacks the depth of Hedley Thomas and Sean Parnell, who have covered the businessman-turned-politician in immense detail in the *Australian* and in an 80,000-word book respectively.

Rundle draws extensively on Parnell's book, *Clive: The story of Clive Palmer*, a fact disclosed about halfway through and in the acknowledgments, and this means there's little new material on Palmer's early life or his present business interests.

Rundle's treatment of Thomas is one of many disappointing aspects of this essay. Thomas, a formidable investigative journalist with five Walkley Awards to his credit, is introduced in such a perfunctory way that readers will see him as a Murdoch hack who does the bidding of his master. Rundle's linking of the coverage by the *Australian*, and Thomas especially, with Palmer's bizarre claim about Rupert Murdoch's ex-wife Wendi Deng being a Chinese government spy is fundamentally flawed and unfair to Thomas.

To set the record straight, Thomas's first big piece about Palmer and his political ambitions was published on 15 June 2013. The article, which carried the headline "Should this man run our nation?", followed Palmer's boast that he would become prime minister.

As the election drew closer, Thomas wrote a steady stream of stories about Palmer, culminating in a front-page article that exposed a series of claims that Palmer had made about being a professor, a G20 adviser, a mining magnate and a billionaire. Palmer made the comment about Deng being a Chinese spy on the day of publication, 5 September, so Thomas's burrowing into Palmer's life was well underway when Palmer made these remarks.

This critique of News Corporation and the *Australian* in particular wouldn't be so ludicrous if Rundle didn't then lambast the media at large for ignoring Palmer. While he says News was "going him ... for going up against Rupert," in the very next breath he says the remainder of the press ignored him "throughout the election campaign and its aftermath." Well, this situation surely underscores the public interest merit of News devoting considerable resources to probing into Palmer's affairs?

Rundle also argues, unconvincingly, that the *Australian*'s focus on Palmer was unfair because commensurate attention was not given to other "politically engaged" rich men, such as James Packer, Frank Lowy and Rupert Murdoch. But Rundle doesn't concede the obvious point that none has a political party with seats in parliament and a potential stranglehold on the Senate.

Paul Cleary

A longer version of this piece was first published in the Weekend Australian on 6 December 2014.

Geoff Robinson

Guy Rundle tells a great story in *Clivosaurus*. It is the story of Clive Palmer, a boy from the Gold Coast who lived the Australian dream of an ample sufficiency and who then became the defender of this dream against Tony Abbott. But like most good writers, Rundle also tells his own story: of a boy from the *Arena*-land of the inner-city left, in search of the suburban and coastal Australian dream – *Upper Middle Bogan* as essay. It is *Coolangatta* to Canberra for Palmer, and Carlton to Carrum for Rundle. Both Rundle and Palmer are nationalist optimists and both diverge from stereotypical images of "left" and "right": Rundle is a longstanding critic of conventional left-libertarianism on issues such as euthanasia, and mining baron Palmer has rallied to the defence of Australian welfarism. That Rundle is fascinated by Palmer is not surprising, but in the end the hopes he places in him are misplaced.

Rundle's fascination is with the *ideal* of Clive Palmer. To Rundle, Palmer's mastery of reinvention makes him a man for the times. Rundle commences with a consideration of the divergence between Palmer's liberal views on the government budget deficit and refugees, and the conservatism of many who voted for him. To Rundle, the pre-election and post-election Palmer are distinct. Palmer's own life story, Rundle contends, has made him someone who can boldly articulate what "Australians owed to each other" within an "overarching moral account" that makes him uniquely suited to be a bearer of the "core values … close to the centre of Australian politics."

After the Abbott government's first budget, many on the left saw their Facebook timelines cluttered by excited shares of Palmer's press conferences. Rundle's essay reflects that time and mood. There is wishful thinking here. Left intellectuals in Australia are usually dissatisfied with "their" parties and regularly offer what they believe to be election-winning advice. Left politicians usually ignore this advice, to their electoral benefit. Rundle seems to leap from the fact that

Palmer provided an obstruction to Tony Abbott to the assumption that somehow his challenge to Abbott resonated with the public. In fact, discontent with Abbott fuelled the rapid political revival of the establishment left, in the form of Labor and the Greens.

Rundle is keen to refute the image of Palmer as an amoral conservative opportunist, but his narrative of Palmer's colourful life story is deeply teleological: Palmer's many identities – Catholic conservative, liberal reformer, romantic poet and mining entrepreneur – are seen to have made him a vessel for particular values. For Rundle, these values are Australian egalitarianism and a Catholic social justice tradition. For all the thick description that Rundle gives us, Palmer remains a shadowy figure in his portrayal. It seems Rundle believes that Palmer's significance is dependent on his ideological depth. This reflects a modernist conception of political life as an intensely serious task. To Rundle, Palmer must have ideological depth to be a significant figure. But Palmer can be all surface, reinvention and appearance, yet also remain deeply significant. Palmer is a postmodern politician whose persona is based on constant reinvention, but his rise and apparent fall speaks to the exhaustion of postmodernity in the age of financial crisis and secular stagnation.

Rundle wants to find a foundation for Palmer, and so he revives the discourses of the early 1990s, when B.A. Santamaria was feted by some on the left as a critic of neoliberalism. To Rundle, Palmer's defence of Australian values reflects a Catholic legacy; Rundle is concerned to enlist Palmer in a familiar crusade against that communitarian/conservative/socialist bogy the "atomised and content-less self of classical liberal doctrine." For Rundle, content and depth are important, and he seeks to persuade readers that Palmer has these qualities.

After the death of socialism, Rundle as a left intellectual finds the model of depth and seriousness in Catholicism. For Rundle, ultimately Palmer's politics are all about the legacy of the 1891 papal encyclical *Rerum Novarum*. But *Rerum Novarum* is like Marx's *Capital*: often cited but rarely read. The encyclical is largely a polemic against socialism, which gives little support to trade unions or the welfare state. Rather like Clive Palmer himself, it is a symbol attached to competing causes. Catholics who faced competition from socialism cited *Rerum Novarum* to justify policies largely identical to those of the moderate left. Catholic unions were not fundamentally different from socialist unions; Australian Labor had an abundance of Catholic leaders, but its practice was distinctly non-Catholic. The significance of the arbitration system lay not in its regulation of wages, but in its promotion of trade unionism. As Peter Lindert shows in his 2004 book *Growing Public*, European political Catholicism did not encourage the growth of the welfare state until after World War II. It was then that European Catholics decided to compete democratically with their rivals to the left rather than exclude them from politics by anti-democratic force. In Australia, B.A. Santamaria took the word of papal encyclicals seriously; for him, this meant opposition to the arbitration system as a promoter of class conflict, together with a deep suspicion of social welfare as an subversion of family responsibilities. Rundle makes much of the living wage as an Australian ideal, but as a principle separate from trade unionism it only arrived in the economically rational 1990s, with the Keating government's 1993 industrial relations reforms.

The Australian values that Rundle evokes may have been a muddled compromise, but they were the result of real social struggles and movements – which no longer exist. But to Rundle, Australian values exist as an eternal identity slumbering in the hearts of citizens. From this perspective, conservative excesses call into automatic existence champions of ordinary life such as Kevin Rudd or Clive Palmer. At times of conservative ascendancy, the Australian left has often rallied to ideals and myths: Russel Ward's evocation of the bush legend during the Menzies era, or Judith Brett's discovery of the moral middle class during the Howard years. In the age of Abbott, Rundle rallies the left by evoking the spirit of the suburbs, as manifest in Clive Palmer. In truth, Australian history is not on the side of the left. *Clivosaurus* tells us much about Clive Palmer, but it tells us more about the contemporary Australian left.

Geoff Robinson

Mark Bahnisch

Guy Rundle, a long-time visitor to the Gold Coast, has captured its ephemerality and shiny emptiness perfectly. A couple of years ago, on the way back to Brisbane from Byron Bay by Greyhound bus, I noticed that many of the '70s hotels and "attractions" had fallen into a state of decay and disorder. Perhaps the action had moved north from the southern end of the coastal strip. Flying back into Coolangatta earlier this year from Singapore, I was amazed that the plane had to be towed to the terminal because of "construction" – a metaphor for the shifting sands of the built environment landwards of the beach. That ugly scenes attend protests against the building of (another) mosque suggests the politics of redevelopment is often nasty, and very much contested. In the recent election campaign, Mermaid Bay MP Ray Stevens astonished most everyone with his silent dance in response to a reporter's questions over his "convergence of interest" as both politician and consultant and investor in a development company. Let's not forget that the man whose spectre looms large over the Coast, Russ Hinze, Minister for Everything under Joh, pioneered both the politics of the land grab and the dodginess that surrounds it. So, if the built environment of the Gold Coast resembles something celebrated in the '70s po-mo architecture tome *Learning from Las Vegas*, its social life seems to reflect that formlessness – the quick road to advancement lies through smarts and quick deals rather than either inherited wealth or constant toil.

It does make sense, then, that Clive learnt how to be Clive on the Goldie.

Let's not forget, either, that Palmer now presides over a dinosaur park and resort on the Sunshine Coast, minutes away from slumbering Mount Coolum. The Gold Coast, as Rundle knows, has always been *sui generis*. Plots hatched there – like the mad "Joh for PM" crusade – have tended to run aground or implode, maybe because the Goldie, a promised land in one sense, has always been a nowhere-land, home to people from elsewhere; it feels simultaneously not-Queensland and hyper-Queensland, utopic and dystopic. Crime stats, particularly those involving violence and guns, are disproportionately bad on the Gold Coast compared to the rest of the state, and Campbell Newman's war on bikies would seem like an overreaction anywhere else.

The Sunshine Coast couldn't be more different, with the exception of the glitzy high-rise and nightclub beachfront of Mooloolaba. Coolum, Peregian and Marcoola beaches are sleepy, Caloundra has more bustle, and Noosa is Noosa — either the Toorak of the North or the Byron Bay of Queensland, depending on your taste and the state of the economy. Buderim is bookshops and Peter Slipper's hideaway house. The south of the Sunshine Coast is non-stop featureless '80s housing estates, but the north is brush and tea-trees, segueing into rainforest. At Maroochydore, over prawns and XXXX, a retired senior sergeant of police once told me that the refugees from Jeff Kennett's Victoria all went bust after buying low-lying land on the flood plains, unawares. I don't know if that's true, but it captures the culture of the place — you win in politics on the Sunshine Coast by promising not to be the Gold Coast. Clive himself ran into much trouble precisely because the dinosaurs, and the land grabs, were more Surfers Paradise than Sunshine Coast. In the hinterland, this is Kevin Rudd country, too, in vibe if not votes, though the old timber-logging town of Eumundi has had an agreeably New Age makeover (and offers yet more bookshops). The Gold Coast, despite the presence of two universities to the Sunshine Coast's one, is not noted for bookshops.

As a bred, if not born, Queenslander myself, I'm much fonder of the Sunny Coast than the Cold Ghost. There's a local identity here, and roots laid down. Sure, there are people from "not round here" (in a Queensland country pub, you're on the outer if you can't claim a family connection), but old British migrants drinking themselves silly at the bowls club fit in well with the local folk. There was never any industry, the banana and strawberry farms are mostly gone, and I've never been able to figure out, while passing through, what most people in places like Buddina do for a living. Maybe the interspersed bottle-os and fundamentalist churches amid the brick-box houses provide a clue, but I'm not sure. Just as with other, more northerly, districts along the sprawling Queensland coastline, average incomes are low. If you drive from Buderim down to Maroochydore, every second house seems to offer knife sharpening or fresh fruit or some other service, usually with a hand-painted sign. There are no doubt dreams dreamt here, but not the sorts of grand ones Clive dreams, which may account for the puzzlement Rundle describes at the bizarre PUP open day. As Rundle also notes, not many of the voters of Fairfax actually cast a first preference vote for the PUP in the person of the sometime professor from Bond University.

Queensland can be relied on to send a shockwave south at least once a decade, albeit one whose impact diminishes the further south it travels. The "Bible-bashing bastard," Joh Bjelke-Petersen, brought down Gough Whitlam in the '70s; with his quixotic campaign for Canberra in the '80s, the newly dubbed Sir Joh crashed and burned John Howard in pre-Lazarus days; Pauline Hanson spread bile from Ipswich in the '90s; and Bob Katter, the Man with the Big White Hat, arguably should have made his run in the 2000s (by the early 2010s, homophobia and anti-Asian prejudice were a mile too far to travel even for many of his natural supporters). Clive's impact seems to follow the same laws of political geographic motion, the wave diminishing to a small stream by the time it hit Victoria. Yet Palmer himself is not a Queenslander by birth, and his joint appearance with Al Gore, his support for solar energy (a mainstay of the party's policies in the Queensland state election), his open mind to open borders for refugees and his support for free tertiary education all seem decidedly un-Queensland. Although his various crazy tax schemes fit the mould. (It would be intriguing to trace the history of eccentric tax policy ideas from Queensland insurgents – they've all, from Joh onwards, had them. Maybe there's a bit of Henry George energy persisting in the backblocks.)

Although the PUP replicated One Nation by being more of an invitation-only club than a political party, it didn't necessarily appeal to the same sorts of voters, many of whom are now, by virtue of the effluxion of time, living in the Lockyer Valley in the Sky. It's possible that Palmer's vote was more the result of inattention than any devotion to a populist cause. He was there, he mailed folks a DVD, and he was neither Labor nor Liberal. Whatever weight one gives to Rundle's picture of the man's political philosophy – and I suspect that it's a little less Rerum Novarum and a little more populism without doctrines than Guy allows – his electoral strength in 2013's federal election is most certainly an expression of anti-politics. Hence too, probably, the weakness of the Palmer push in Queensland this year. So much for destroying Newman; maybe that task was delegated to Alan Jones. The PUP style in 2015 is more of a Twitter feed than a campaign.

The key to all this might be the impossibility of translating anti-politics into politics. Rundle makes much of Palmer actually playing politics – dealing, negotiating, feinting, seizing the high ground, retreating. That is what he was doing, and that was what the serried ranks of the press gallery and the political class and big business decried as "instability." That's all true, but the dilemma for any anti-politician who succeeds in entering politics is that they then become, ipso facto, a politician. There is another way – the Beppe Grillo or Sinn Fein model – a politics of parliamentary abstention or abstentionism. Get elected, don't follow the logic. But for any populist or anti-political movement desirous of exercising power, whether it's the UK Independence Party, Podemos in Spain, Syriza in Greece, the Tea Party in the US, or the PUP in Australia, traps loom. Palmer might have done better to have followed the first path: decry and denounce everything and force a double dissolution, knocking the Coalition for six and improving his parliamentary representation as a bonus.

I have argued elsewhere that the rise of populism and anti-politics has three key antecedents: deep globalisation, changes in opportunity structures and the liquidity of our lives, and the information revolution. Anti-politics, and the decay of politics and the political class, is often ascribed to the fracturing of the social bases political parties have long relied on for legitimacy, and a consequent system crisis. That's true, but it's not the whole story.

Here, the Queensland phenomenon is illuminating. If the key divide in Australian politics in the twentieth century was between an industrial working class and a capitalist class, that wasn't the picture in the Sunshine State. There was little heavy manufacturing; the unions had their strength in the bush; and mining, transport and construction more often recruited short-term, contract and seasonal workers than lifers. Liberals were weak, resting only on the Brisbane legal and medical professions, and big business was always from "somewhere else" – interstate, if not the American and Japanese capital so warmly embraced by Joh. Rural life was protected by complex marketing and distribution mechanisms, boards, single desks and the panoply of agrarian socialism, while Queensland was very much a free-trade state compared to Victoria, with its industrial protectionism. In this environment, and in a massive landmass overlayed by multiple regional politics (small-scale settlement versus grazing country, red earth versus scrub – a lot more complicated than just urban versus rural), we had something like a three-party system, with the Liberals always squeezed in between Labor and the Country/National parties, whose dominance lasted for decades. Why? More because they represented a certain authoritarian mode of "strong" governance than because of the social interests on which their bases were built.

It's a bit like that now – Labor and the LNP are just there, the default choices, offered up by a political system that privileges organisational and financial strength over genuine representation. "Interests" are also missing in action: an economy that creates short-term and contract work, and a culture that encourages constant changes of tack and career – neither lends themselves to the commonality of lived experience that saw majorities unionised. On the other side of the coin, the fluidity, impermanence and globality of capital gives the lie to the picture of a coherent Australian capitalist class, an ideological confection if there ever was one. Australia, I would argue, is becoming more Queensland, and thus Clive Palmer had his chance. Just as Kevin came from Queensland to help, so too did Clive, but no one was really looking for the sort of help on offer, if that manifested as horse-trading in the Senate rather than giving voice to the sense that politics was alien, meaningless, something to be managed as part of the struggle for existence rather than something of clear and present import. Clive Palmer's political epitaph might be: "he was just another politician." As Rundle no doubt sees clearly now, that leaves us in a nowhere-land not dissimilar to the illusory glamour of the Gold Coast.

Mark Bahnisch

Dennis Atkins

Clive Palmer didn't appear at his eponymous political party's launch for the late January Queensland state election, leaving the introductions to Senator Glenn Lazarus. As usual, it was a very yellow affair, with the candidates given Palmer United Party canary-coloured corflutes to hand out to the ageing Sunshine Coast audience. The event was held in a fairly modest function room at the Palmer Coolum Resort on a Sunday morning – it was just finishing as Campbell Newman took to the stage at the Brisbane Convention & Exhibition Centre for his big campaign rally. The star turn was the PUP state leader, John Bjelke-Petersen, son of the former, mostly discredited, premier, the late Sir Joh, and his remarkable wife, the former senator, Flo.

John, who has a face every bit as crumpled as his dad's, was ushered in to the pumping disco sound and menacing refrain of "Eye of the Tiger." Like most things Clive, John's speech defied logic and stereotype. There was a mix of pro-business free enterprise, some early twentieth-century state intervention, an astonishing call to keep the police out of politics (did a Bjelke-Petersen really say that?) and a jumble of federal, state and local government complaints.

It was hard to tell how much advance notice the PUP state leader had of his speech's content – at one stage he laughed at the end of a joke line as if it was the first time he'd read it – but he did manage to get to the end, prompting a burst of sign-waving, fist-pumping and hip-swinging that momentarily transformed the room into something resembling a Zumba session at a gated community.

John Bjelke-Petersen never had a chance in the state election, taking on Deputy Premier Jeff Seeney in the rural Central Queensland seat of Callide, with its 23 per cent buffer. The other PUP candidates – even those standing on the Gold and Sunshine coasts, where Palmer has his strongest, still waning, support – never had a hope either, in a contest that increasingly polarised voters. Even Palmer, who spent much of the campaign out of the country, didn't seem to have his heart in it. There were only a handful of the big yellow billboards – once so prevalent they looked more like street signs in some neighbourhoods – here and there on the coasts.

The 2015 Queensland election might be seen as the beginning of the end for PUP, although Clive has half a term to run as the member for Fairfax and his remaining two senators, Lazarus and Perth's Dio Wang, are there for five more years. The irony of the PUP's failure to win seats or do any real damage to the Newman government in the polls – it was doing enough damage to itself, as it happened – is that the party was established as a vehicle for payback against the Liberal National Party in Queensland. The foray into federal politics was designed as a curtain-raiser for the main event in Queensland. But it appears that the first act was as good as it got.

Guy Rundle's essay accurately traces the roots of Palmer's political involvement to the rise of the business-as-politics model that grew up while Sir Joh was premier and ministers like Russ Hinze corrupted public life. Palmer's flirtation with the Nationals dates to a time when the party had Country as its name – he was hired as a campaign assistant in the very early '70s, but after six months, party boss Bob Sparkes showed him the door. Clive's return coincided with the "Joh for PM" push, a serious attempt by a group of wealthy developers to buy a government, and his disaffection with the LNP followed a falling out over money, not policy.

The Palmer political model, built with cash and supported by a membership often indistinguishable from the party leader's own interests, is not sustainable. It has no core beliefs beyond Hallmark platitudes and Wikipedia definitions of democracy. When the crossover between Palmer's private and corporate ambitions and his political manoeuvring becomes so apparent and contradictory it can't be hidden, the public attraction fades. Palmer won't be the last to use wealth and baloney to curry political favour – the internet age is made for him and his like – but it looks like his time is running out.

Dennis Atkins

Malcolm Mackerras

According to my assessment, Australia has a dozen psephologists: eleven men and one woman, South Australia's Jenni Newton-Farrelly. If we rank these twelve people from most advocating reform to least advocating reform, we would have Rundle at one extreme and myself at the other. Australia's current best-known and most prolific psephologist, Antony Green, would be placed halfway between us.

I accept Rundle's claim that all his advocacy of reform is based on democratic principles, and I would assert that of myself also. I would not say that about Green. In my view, his advocacy of reform is based on the idea that Australia has three worthy parties — the Liberal Party, the Australian Labor Party and the Greens — and ten unworthy parties: the National Party, the Family First Party, the Palmer United Party, the Liberal Democratic Party, the Shooters and Fishers Party, the Australian Motoring Enthusiast Party, the Australian Sex Party, the Dignity for Disability party, the Democratic Labour Party and the Vote 1 Local Jobs party. According to Green's view (at least as I interpret it), these latter parties get their seats in state upper houses by gaming the system. If they do not actually engage in that nasty practice themselves, they defend electoral systems that help other unworthy parties to engage in that practice.

Let me consider a case to illustrate my point. In March 2014 the Labor government of Jay Weatherill won a South Australian general election by gaming the system. Then, in December, it converted its win as a minority government into a majority, by the luck of winning the electoral district of Fisher at a by-election. It did that after winning a mere 47 per cent of the two-party preferred vote in March, compared with 53 per cent won by the Liberal Party. How would these three psephologists react to that?

Rundle would say, "Yes, of course it was a case of Labor gaming the system. It is a rotten system which must be abandoned in favour of proportional representation." I would say, "Yes, of course it was a case of Labor gaming the system, but radical change is not needed. At some future date, South Australia will get a government not tainted as being illegitimate." Meanwhile, Green would not say that Labor gamed the system at all. For him, the only ones "gaming the system" – to gain their upper house seats – are those parties he deems unworthy.

However, coming back to Rundle, I wish to refute any suggestion by him or anyone else that any of the three PUP senators could be said to be in the Senate courtesy of their gaming the system. It is true, however, that none of them received a quota on the first count.

Glenn Lazarus received 9.9 per cent in Queensland, which is a high number, more than two-thirds of a quota. No one has suggested that there was anything unfair about his election.

Jacqui Lambie received 6.6 per cent in Tasmania. Hers was a low absolute number of votes because Tasmania is our least populous state. Yet we have all these people (mainly in the business community) calling for a threshold. The standard demand is for 5 per cent, as in New Zealand. Lambie would have been elected even if there had been a 5 per cent threshold. Green has written that the third Liberal candidate, Sally Chandler, was democratically entitled to the seat. His argument is that the Liberal Party group won 2.63 quotas, while the PUP group won only 0.46 of a quota. That is a reasonable proposition, I suppose. However, Australia has a candidate-based electoral system and the first preference vote for Lambie was 21,794, while that for Chandler was 637. It could be said that both Lambie and Chandler engaged in preference harvesting, but Lambie was more successful. She finished with 55,571 votes, compared to 39,906 for Chandler.

Before I consider the case of Dio Wang, I ask myself: why do we have a candidate-based electoral system? To that question, I answer: because our constitution commands it. Section 7 of the Australian Constitution states: "The Senate shall be composed of senators for each State, directly chosen by the people of the State, voting … as one electorate." Were we to have a party-list system (as New Zealand has for its House of Representatives), our politicians would not be "directly chosen by the people." They would be appointed by party machines. The role of the electorate under a party-list system is merely to distribute numbers of seats among the parties according to their proportions of the effective votes. I say "effective votes," because many votes are thrown into the rubbish bin by the thresholds that apply in such systems.

Reverting to Clive Palmer, however, the most interesting case of his senators is Wang in Western Australia. In respect of the September 2013 election, he received exactly 5 per cent of the formal vote and was not declared elected. So he appealed to the High Court sitting as the Court of Disputed Returns. Justice Kenneth Hayne, being the court, declared the entire election void and ordered a re-run. At that election, Wang received 12.3 per cent, which was quite close to the quota of 14.3 per cent. No one has suggested that there was anything unfair about the result of the West Australian supplementary election.

Not only were the elections of these three senators (Lazarus, Lambie and Wang) fair, but the entire election result was fair.

Rundle finishes his section "Gaming the System" with this comment on page 65:

> Palmer's invocation of a centrist politics with strong roots in Australian political tradition came at a time when there was mass opposition to the budget that was attacking such measures, but an inability by Labor to give an overarching moral account of why such a budget was wrong. Clive Palmer could, but what he couldn't do was switch out of the clownish mode that he had used to gain publicity during and after the 2013 election. That failure to project a more consistent and reasoned political style may have cost him his best chance to convert his freak win at the craps table of Australian democracy into a broader political movement.

I agree with that. Palmer engaged in a gamble. Just what else is new? His gamble came off, because he was elected as one of 150 members in the House of Representatives and he was able to get three senators elected – and their success fairly closely matched their share of the vote. The system, therefore, does not deserve the derision to which Rundle subjects it. Every election under every system is, to some extent, a crapshoot.

I come now to the final section of the essay, "Of Dinosaurs and Democracy." In it, Rundle describes a highly unlikely outcome to the 2016 federal election and then goes on:

> Maybe it will take an event of that magnitude to shake us from our complacency, our mistaking of torpor and disengagement for orderliness and legitimacy. If so, bring it on. But it would be better to start a conversation now, a real one, ranging across the country, about what sort of changes would make for a genuinely representative and more democratic system. That would involve discussion of multi-member electorates, voluntary voting, list systems, optional

preferentiality, Senate thresholds, campaign spending, different models of public funding or its abolition altogether, the role of the governor-general, and beyond. Some of these measures face the near-impossible hurdle of a referendum, but many can be achieved by legislation. The most democratic way to re-ground Australian democracy would be for a series of such conversations to lead to a non-binding national plebiscite on proposals to reform our democracy, the results of which would guide subsequent bills in parliament. Any party that set itself against a manifest desire for change would expose itself as more committed to the system than to the popular will.

Sorry, Guy, but I cannot agree with that. For a start, half of those proposals would require changes to the Constitution. Not that I want to get into an argument on that. If the scenario you paint were to occur at the federal level, the reaction would be the same as was the case for that South Australian election, mentioned above. Perhaps there would be some tinkering. But it would be much more likely that the losers would say, "We have accepted this system, so we are willing to let the chips fall where they may."

As a postscript, I note that earlier, while defending the South Australian electoral system, I wrote, "At some future date South Australia will get a government not tainted as being illegitimate." As I wrote those words, I did not realise just how quickly I would be proved right. However, I insist that I have been proved right. Quite apart from the Fisher by-election, we had a Newspoll published in the *Australian* newspaper on 31 December 2014. It showed the distribution of the two-party-preferred vote as 53/47 in Labor's favour, compared with the reverse at the March general election. So, even with a result like that, and even with Labor's naked gaming of the system, there is now a government in South Australia enjoying every bit as much legitimacy as the governments of all the other jurisdictions.

Malcolm Mackerras

Grant Agnew

On page 47 of *Clivosaurus*, Guy Rundle shows that he too is unaware of an important political change. He refers to an "idea implicit in the bicameral system: that the upper house should review legislation but ultimately show regard for the fact that the public had chosen a government, with a program, in the lower house." This idea has been dead and gone for nearly five years, killed off by Tony Abbott.

In February 2010, Kevin Rudd had a mandate for his emissions trading scheme – it had been an election promise in 2007. Back then, though, the Senate was controlled by the Liberals and a Christian fellow traveller of theirs who had about as much real support as Ricky Muir has now. At the start of the 2010 parliamentary year, Tony Abbott stood in front of TV cameras and said, "The government has its policies but we have ours, and we will be pursuing them through the Senate." Everyone knows what happened after that.

Since 1 July 2014, the new Senate has been out of anyone's control, and all of the non-government parties are simply doing to Abbott what in 2010 he said was right and proper. This includes Clive Palmer's deal-making. Abbott has no grounds for complaint, and the commentariat should be telling him so. It should not support any whining from Abbott (or Christopher Pyne, or Joe Hockey, or Mathias Cormann, Eric Abetz, George Brandis and so on) about mandates and election promises and other such things which the Liberals have casually treated as complete crap.

What should be said instead is, "Be careful about what you wish for, Tony, because you might get it."

We can't expect Murdoch or Fairfax writers to say that, though. The really odd thing here is that in the bitchy, childish, poisoned atmosphere which Abbott and his mob have created, the likes of Guy Rundle don't say it either.

Grant Agnew

Guy Rundle

Some months after *Clivosaurus* came out, *The Chaser*'s Dominic Knight suggested that it be put online and updated daily. At least. Since the essay was published, Palmer has suffered a loss of control of the crossbench balance of power in the Senate, with the departure of Jacqui Lambie from the Palmer United Party; has become bogged down in an unedifying court battle with Citic about $12 million paid to Mineralogy and used for PUP electioneering; and, in a pre-Christmas act of gonzo generosity, has seen his media advisor, A. Crook, charged with involvement in the kidnapping of a National Australia Bank employee. Great times, but we may not see their like again.

Palmer's loss of a solid bloc under his command has left him a diminished figure, and as he quit the stage, Tony Abbott returned to start the new year off by knighting Prince Philip. This stunning act has made the essay a snapshot of a period: that year or so when all the crazy was with the crossbenches, and the most erratic member of parliament was someone other than the prime minister.

By the time Palmer lost control of the commanding heights, however, he had all but ensured that the government's budget lay in ruins, that their plans for a Medicare co-payment would not go ahead, and that attempts to impose higher university fees would not pass. The Abbott government had hoped it could get its horror budget through quickly and minimise the backlash. The budget's sequestration in the Senate allowed dissent to build to the point where it undermined support for the government, to a disastrous degree; it was in this context that Abbott's knighting of Sir Prince Philip became not just another idiosyncrasy, but a measure of failure and delusion on the part of the PM, and the party started down the road to a spill and, according to commentators across the spectrum, Abbott's near-certain political demise in the coming months. Say what one will about Clive Palmer, he has had a historical effect.

Whether that has ended, or whether Clive has a few shots left in the locker, remains to be seen. My hope, expressed in the essay, was that Clive's greatest impact might be on our ossified and unexamined political system, by bringing closer a crisis in its operation, such that we would have to do something about it. Few reviewers and commentators bothered to attend to this part of the essay (an important exception was Tim Dunlop on the ABC's opinion website, *The Drum*), even though it seemed to me the crucial point for the future.

The election of Clive Palmer was an effect of our current political system, and revealed its ramshackle nature; now that Palmer was a power in the land, it might be worth knowing who he was and how he saw the world – these were the themes of the essay that some respondents have commented on. Others appear to have had handy suggestions for the essay I should have written, and wilfully or otherwise missed or misconstrued my argument.

The easiest ones to deal with are those that complement or amplify the essay, and I thank Richard Denniss, Mark Bahnisch and Dennis Atkins for their contributions. Grant Agnew notes that Abbott had repudiated the notion of the Senate as subordinate to the House before the PUP struck out on an independent course. Fair enough, but the Senate's role has often been more honoured in the breach than the observance, and I was simply noting that Palmer was to some degree honouring it.

Paul Cleary, a part-time staff writer for the *Australian*, takes the Baader-Meinhof approach to criticism and makes his sole mission the recovery of captured comrades – in this case, the writers I criticised for simply slamming Palmer when it was clear he had become a problem for Tony Abbott, a man for whom they had some regard at the time. But it's a writer I didn't criticise whom I am pilloried most for mistreating. Cleary thinks that much of the essay should have focused on Hedley Thomas's story about Palmer's fast and loose use of $12 million from Citic for electoral purposes, and that to not do so was disrespectful. Since I had acknowledged that Thomas's story was "legitimate and necessary" and since it was his story, and I duly included it, it's hard to see the strength of the objection. The essay is about who Clive Palmer might be and the situation in which he came to sudden power. Once the Citic story was noted, there wasn't much to say about it: although juicy for daily coverage, it didn't have that much content. Indeed, between the publication of the essay and the reviews, Palmer paid back the cash, and there remains only a ridiculous residual lawsuit about interest on the money and legal costs, with the Chinese attempting to push for a fraud finding – despite the judge threatening to throw out the case because both parties were using Australian courts as a "plaything." It's a non-starter, unless, like too many *Australian* journalists, you have an obsessive interest in the scoop, however minor, and little or none in the deeper currents of life.

As regards Malcolm Mackerras's stoush with Antony Green, I think I'll just hold the coats. On the essay itself, Mackerras engages in a fairly comprehensive misrepresentation. He says that I accused PUP of gaming the system. I did nothing of the sort. I said that since the introduction of above-the-line Senate voting, there had been potential for the system to be (legally) gamed – which it has been, by the micro-parties – but I did not accuse the PUP of doing this. It did benefit from being part of the preference cycles that the micro-parties had had engineered, but the PUP ran as a full, upfront party. It won because it had millions of dollars to play with, but that little bit of non-democracy is a different issue. Mackerras then asserts that I have suggested the system is broken because the PUP gained four seats in 2013. No, I argued that any system which regularly gives a majority of seats, and government, to a party gaining a minority of votes, is broken, and to be okay with that is a form of cynicism to be found in abundance among political professionals. Mackerras is not only opposed to any change in the system, he also opposes my suggestion that we have a national conversation about it. He does not even want to defend the status quo he supports. Given what an obvious racket it is, I don't blame him.

Geoff Robinson exaggerates my interpretation of Clive in order to argue that I construe him as some sort of culture hero, and that I see myself in him. In arguing that Palmer was to some important degree formed by the Catholicism of his mother, a faith he still observes, I attribute a depth to him that he does not possess. Furthermore, in seeing that Catholicism as putting him in a dynamic relationship with the core of Australian political life, I attribute far too much to *Rerum Novarum*, and its relationship to the Harvester judgment, and the tradition that arose from it.

My argument was made in the teeth of incomprehension from the press gallery as to Palmer's motives and course of action. What would he do next? He was crazy, he was without content! It's a judgment Robinson endorses, calling Clive "postmodern." From both parties, that seems a cop-out. My argument was that Palmer's actions – both what he was blocking and what he was letting through – led one to conclude that his politics were still steered by Catholic notions of social responsibility. From that one could predict that he would not deal on the co-payment, and give little ground on university fees. Thus it proved, and the co-payment is dead. To suggest that this is teleological is circular logic: Robinson believes Palmer has no content, is not steered by any deeper beliefs, so any accumulation of evidence that he is and has been must be retroactive speculation.

That seems typical of the refusal of Australian political commentators to interpret political figures – to see them as no more than point particles, and wander around blind. I wanted to work out what Palmer's beliefs were, and what he might do next. Robinson falsely accuses me of building up Palmer into a culture hero, when much of the essay is devoted to making fun of his serial enthusiasms and to concluding that he is a "foolish, passionate man" with limited insight into his own compulsions. On that basis, Robinson then mounts a rather tired Labourist critique of my position on the non-Labor left. This – which seems to be the point of his reply – can only be done by ignoring my main point, acknowledged by other respondents, that I see Palmer as largely an effect of an electoral system which has become dysfunctional. In his rush to caricature by attributing a position to me, vis-à-vis Labor and mainstream politics, that I have not held for some years, and do not express here, he has mangled the evidence. Also his own: the assertion that the "living wage" did not play a role in Australian politics until the 1990s is an embarrassment.

Tietze, from a different tradition, argues that Palmer and the PUP emerged because traditional major-party politics has been hollowed out over the past twenty years. He sees small parties as the beneficiaries of this fragmentation, and includes the Greens in their number. "It is impossible to understand Palmer and the PUP" without an excursion into the details of that process, he notes. Well, it is if you want to keep an essay to 20,000 words and focus on the novel parts of the process, rather than rehashing the Hawke/Keating Accord years. Tietze's version is simplistic, oriented to base-and-class processes, and he entirely fails to take account of the structural complexities I noted: that whatever transformations of the class and party system are occurring, our electoral structure keeps the parties in place, reproducing quasi-autonomously. The Greens are not simply a party accruing disaffected voters; they have taken the stable third-party slot that has been part of Australian politics since the emergence of the DLP in the 1950s. Yet the class/social base of that third party has changed entirely, and my argument is that the Greens represent a class of culture and knowledge producers, whose formation and interests are now distinct from Labor's.

To take the 5 per cent the PUP managed to shave off as some sort of crisis of the system is silly. Tietze's lack of interest in "superstructure" (in the old money) means that he never tackles the salient fact about the Australian political system: its aforementioned capacity to reproduce itself. There is plenty of cynicism, dissatisfaction and apathy in the electorate, but very little evidence of the assertive anti-political mood Tietze seeks. His suggestion that Palmer's attack on the budget was "anti-political" is ludicrous – either that or the term "anti-political" is stretched so wide as to have no usefulness. Palmer may have couched his opposition to the budget in folksy terms – the old ladies in Maroochydore who could no longer afford a trip to the movies – but that is simply political effectiveness. It's what Labor politicians once did. His was a recognisable appeal to equality, tapping into established traditions.

"Anti-politics" serves for Tietze as a substitute for a missing Left, external to the system. In reality, it is a substitute for an accurate explanation of the rise of the Greens. Green parties overseas – in Canada and Ireland, for example – have become more economically liberal as the New Left groupings that founded them die away and their base becomes a prosperous cultural/knowledge producer class. There is an evidentiary test here: if the Greens grow as that class grows, and claim a larger share of it, that will confirm the hypothesis. If they suffer sudden losses of votes – for more than a single election – to upstart new groupings, then the anti-politics model will be vindicated to a degree. I see no sign, in the growth of the Greens over the last fifteen years, that they represent any sort of fragment or substitution or anti-politics rather than an emergent class–party dyad in their own right. The suggestion that the party has not grown stronger in exactly the areas inhabited by the class I'm describing is absurd; the Greens have flourished when they have focused resources on these areas and groups, rather than making a more general appeal.

Tietze disdains any transformation of the electoral/institutional system as trivial, a position you can only take if you see it as a mere shadow of a "real" process. But you don't have to believe that institutional reform is a *sufficient* thing to think that it is necessary or desirable. His disdain leads Tietze into simple obtuseness when he notes that my sketch of a 2016 scenario – in which Tony Abbott is done out of the premiership by a divergence between raw votes and seats, and a clutch of independents – is a repetition of the 2010 election. Yes, that's the point, it is. Surely a Marxist should recognise the importance of a repeated event, and its non-singular meaning. Finally, having suggested that the PUP represents something of a social expression, Tietze sees the collapse of its balance-of-power role as symptomatic – and argues that this somehow invalidates the entire essay. Since I never made any claims that Palmer could keep the show on the road, and I noted that he had squandered his chance of consolidating support by staying with the clown act, with decline likely, it is hard to see how the departure of Jacqui Lambie invalidates the argument, or is expressive of any social process at all.

It's my contention that the rise and fall of the PUP has occurred at an independent level of political action, as an institutional effect, but that its leader may be a man whose make-up and ideas are worth thinking about, if only to try to work out what he's going to do next. Had the Coalition leaders taken up my interpretation, they would have abandoned the co-payment and other measures months before they did, and might have been back on track before the Sir Prince Philip disaster. Had they taken up the mélange of ideas expressed by my detractors – well, they did. They wandered around without any thought as to what the PUP might be or who Clive was, and they got shellacked, again. There's a lot of it about.

Guy Rundle

Grant Agnew lives in Brisbane, where he enjoys retirement.

Dennis Atkins is the *Courier-Mail*'s national affairs editor and writer of the 'Party Games' column, which has been a feature in the paper since the late 1990s. He also has a regular spot on ABC TV's *Insiders*.

Mark Bahnisch is a sociologist and writer. He founded the popular progressive blog Larvatus Prodeo. His book *Everything You Need to Know About Queensland But Were Afraid To Ask* will be published by NewSouth in 2015.

Paul Cleary is a senior writer with the *Australian* and the author of four books, including *Too Much Luck* and *Mine-Field*.

Richard Denniss is an economist and the executive director of the Australia Institute. He contributes columns to the *Canberra Times* and the *Australian Financial Review* and has co-authored *Affluenza*, *An Introduction to Australian Public Policy: Theory and practice* and the forthcoming *Minority Policy: Rethinking government when parliament matters* (with Brenton Prosser).

Karen Hitchcock is the author of the award-winning story collection *Little White Slips* and a regular contributor to the *Monthly*. She is also a staff physician at a large city public hospital.

Malcolm Mackerras was honoured with an AO in 2006; the citation referred to his "commitment to reform and improvement of the electoral system." Aged seventy-five, he is a visiting fellow at the Australian Catholic University in Canberra.

Geoff Robinson is senior lecturer in politics and Australian studies at Deakin University, Geelong. He is the author of *When the Labor Party Dreams: Class, politics and policy in New South Wales, 1930–32*.

Guy Rundle is Crikey's correspondent-at-large. A frequent contributor to a range of publications in Australia and the UK, he was editor of *Arena Magazine* for fifteen years. He has written several hit stage shows for Max Gillies and is the author of, among others, Quarterly Essay 3, *The Opportunist*, *Down to the Crossroads*, an account of the 2008 US presidential election, and *Inland Empire*.

Tad Tietze is a Sydney psychiatrist who co-runs the political blog Left Flank. He was co-editor (with Elizabeth Humphrys and Guy Rundle) of *On Utøya: Anders Breivik, Right terror, racism and Europe*. He has written for a wide variety of publications on politics, psychiatry and electronic music.

SUBSCRIBE to Quarterly Essay & SAVE over 35% on the cover price

Subscriptions: Receive a discount and never miss an issue. Mailed direct to your door.

☐ **1 year subscription** (4 issues): $59 within Australia incl. GST. Outside Australia $89.

☐ **2 year subscription** (8 issues): $105 within Australia incl. GST. Outside Australia $165.

* All prices include postage and handling.

Back Issues: (Prices include postage and handling.)

☐ **QE 2** ($15.99) John Birmingham *Appeasing Jakarta*
☐ **QE 4** ($15.99) Don Watson *Rabbit Syndrome*
☐ **QE 6** ($15.99) John Button *Beyond Belief*
☐ **QE 7** ($15.99) John Martinkus *Paradise Betrayed*
☐ **QE 8** ($15.99) Amanda Lohrey *Groundswell*
☐ **QE 10** ($15.99) Gideon Haigh *Bad Company*
☐ **QE 11** ($15.99) Germaine Greer *Whitefella Jump Up*
☐ **QE 12** ($15.99) David Malouf *Made in England*
☐ **QE 13** ($15.99) Robert Manne with David Corlett *Sending Them Home*
☐ **QE 14** ($15.99) Paul McGeough *Mission Impossible*
☐ **QE 15** ($15.99) Margaret Simons *Latham's World*
☐ **QE 17** ($15.99) John Hirst *"Kangaroo Court"*
☐ **QE 18** ($15.99) Gail Bell *The Worried Well*
☐ **QE 19** ($15.99) Judith Brett *Relaxed & Comfortable*
☐ **QE 20** ($15.99) John Birmingham *A Time for War*
☐ **QE 21** ($15.99) Clive Hamilton *What's Left?*
☐ **QE 22** ($15.99) Amanda Lohrey *Voting for Jesus*
☐ **QE 23** ($15.99) Inga Clendinnen *The History Question*
☐ **QE 24** ($15.99) Robyn Davidson *No Fixed Address*
☐ **QE 25** ($15.99) Peter Hartcher *Bipolar Nation*
☐ **QE 26** ($15.99) David Marr *His Master's Voice*
☐ **QE 27** ($15.99) Ian Lowe *Reaction Time*
☐ **QE 28** ($15.99) Judith Brett *Exit Right*
☐ **QE 29** ($15.99) Anne Manne *Love & Money*

☐ **QE 30** ($15.99) Paul Toohey *Last Drinks*
☐ **QE 31** ($15.99) Tim Flannery *Now or Never*
☐ **QE 32** ($15.99) Kate Jennings *American Revolution*
☐ **QE 33** ($15.99) Guy Pearse *Quarry Vision*
☐ **QE 34** ($15.99) Annabel Crabb *Stop at Nothing*
☐ **QE 36** ($15.99) Mungo MacCallum *Australian Story*
☐ **QE 37** ($15.99) Waleed Aly *What's Right?*
☐ **QE 38** ($15.99) David Marr *Power Trip*
☐ **QE 39** ($15.99) Hugh White *Power Shift*
☐ **QE 42** ($15.99) Judith Brett *Fair Share*
☐ **QE 43** ($15.99) Robert Manne *Bad News*
☐ **QE 44** ($15.99) Andrew Charlton *Man-Made World*
☐ **QE 45** ($15.99) Anna Krien *Us and Them*
☐ **QE 46** ($15.99) Laura Tingle *Great Expectations*
☐ **QE 47** ($15.99) David Marr *Political Animal*
☐ **QE 48** ($15.99) Tim Flannery *After the Future*
☐ **QE 49** ($15.99) Mark Latham *Not Dead Yet*
☐ **QE 50** ($15.99) Anna Goldsworthy *Unfinished Business*
☐ **QE 51** ($15.99) David Marr *The Prince*
☐ **QE 52** ($15.99) Linda Jaivin *Found in Translation*
☐ **QE 53** ($15.99) Paul Toohey *That Sinking Feeling*
☐ **QE 54** ($15.99) Andrew Charlton *Dragon's Tail*
☐ **QE 55** ($15.99) Noel Pearson *A Rightful Place*
☐ **QE 56** ($15.99) Guy Rundle *Clivosaurus*

Payment Details: I enclose a cheque/money order made out to Schwartz Publishing Pty Ltd. Please debit my credit card (Mastercard or Visa accepted).

Card No.

Expiry date / **CCV** **Amount $**

Cardholder's name **Signature**

Name

Address

Email **Phone**

Post or fax this form to: Quarterly Essay, Reply Paid 79448, Collingwood VIC 3066 / Tel: (03) 9486 0288 / Fax: (03) 9486 0244 / Email: subscribe@blackincbooks.com
Subscribe online at **www.quarterlyessay.com**